NORTH CAROLINA
STATE BOARD OF COMMUNITY COLLEGES
LIBRARY
WAKE TECHNICAL COMMUNITY COLLEGE

BEGINNING THE NOVEL

Peter Porosky
University of Maryland

UNIVERSITY
PRESS OF
AMERICA

Lanham • New York • London

Copyright © 1994 by
University Press of America®, Inc.
4720 Boston Way
Lanham, Maryland 20706

3 Henrietta Street
London WC2E 8LU England

All rights reserved
Printed in the United States of America
British Cataloging in Publication Information Available

Library of Congress Cataloging-in-Publication Data
Porosky, P.H.
Beginning the novel / by Peter Porosky.
p. cm.
Includes bibliographical references and index.
1. Fiction – Technique.   I. Title.
PN3365.P67   1994   808.3–dc20   94-8397   CIP

ISBN 0–8191–9501–4 (cloth : alk. paper)
ISBN 0–8191–9502–2 (pbk. : alk. paper)

 The paper used in this publication meets the minimum requirements of American National Standard for Information Sciences—Permanence of Paper for Printed Library Materials, ANSI Z39.48–1984.

for Jim Hall

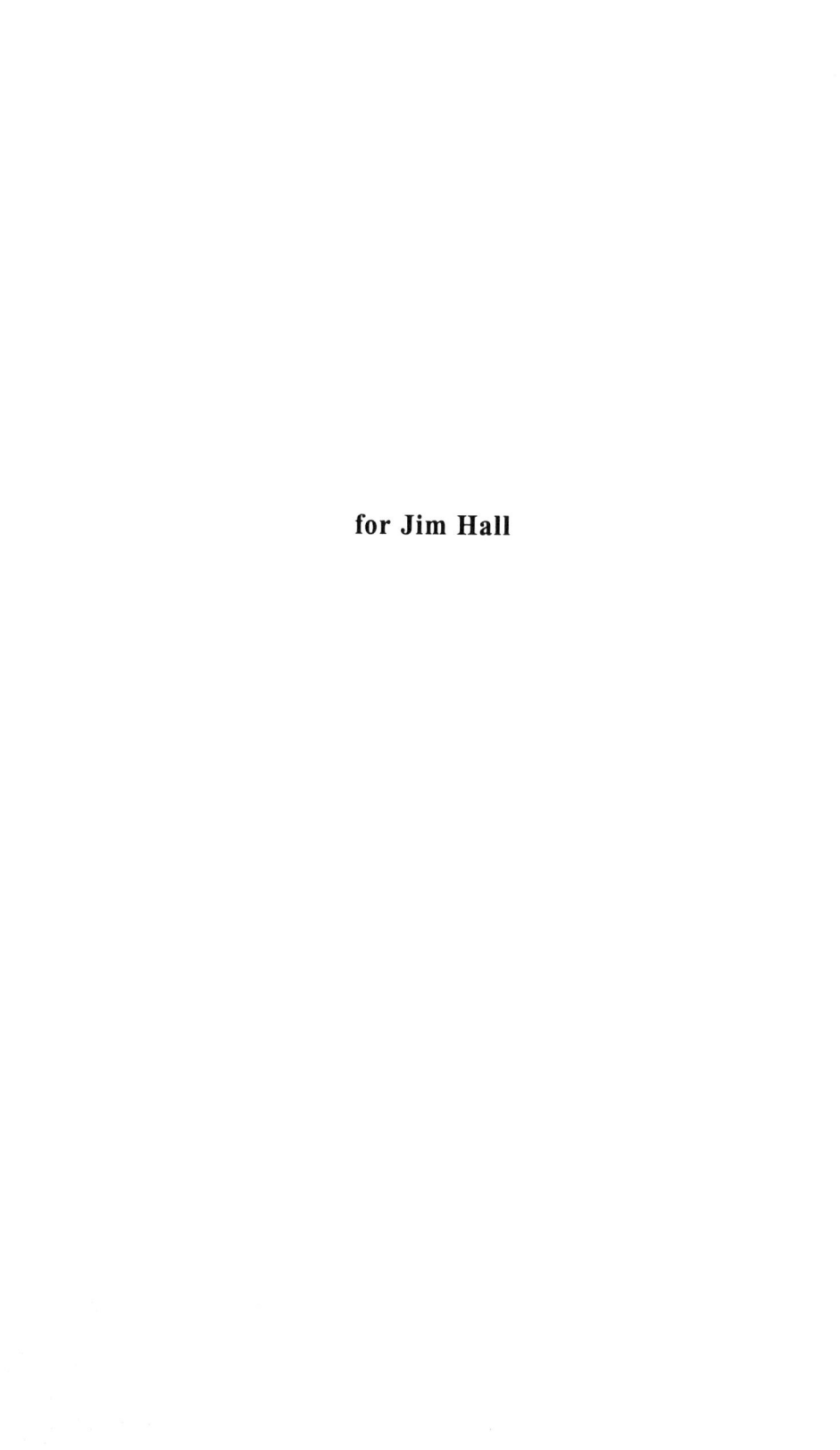

Contents

STEP ONE
[The Process] 1
STEP TWO
[The Techniques] 7
STEP THREE
[The Idea] 25
STEP FOUR
 [The Characters] 37
STEP FIVE
[The Story] 47
STEP SIX
[The Plot Structure] 55
STEP SEVEN
[The Plot Elements] 65
STEP EIGHT
[The Complete Blocking Out] 73
STEP NINE
[The Opening Chapter] 81
STEP TEN
[The Rest of the Novel] 89
Appendix A
Marketing Your Novel 103
Appendix B
Bibliography 107
Appendix C
Glossary 110
Index 116

ACKNOWLEDGEMENTS

I would like to thank the following people whose loving assistance and considerable expertise made this book possible:

Linda Kremer-Porosky
Don Carl Steffen
Don and Barb DeMark
Allan Lefcowitz
Jane Fox
Members of the Sligo Creek Writers' Group

Fyodor Dostoevsky was an obsessive gambler and suffered from at least two major illnesses.

STEP ONE

[The Process]

Task Procedure:

Commit to the process of writing a novel.

You're looking at this book because something about writing a novel interests you. Maybe you've always wanted to write a novel, but never had the time, never thought you could, or never really knew how to get started. Maybe you've already tried to write a novel and didn't finish it. Maybe you've written one or more novels, and they're sitting in a drawer or closet right now because no one would publish them. If one of these scenarios is close to your situation, you're not alone. It doesn't take much intelligence to realize what the successful publication of your novel would do for your life. At the very least, you would gain a great sense of achievement, and at the most, you might become rich! But right about now, you're already beginning to discount the possibility, thinking of reasons why you really can't fulfill this lifelong, secret dream.

There are countless books with all kinds of intriguing titles which make you pick them up with the same hope that you picked up this one. I know. I've read most of them. And they failed me like they failed you. Why? Because they were not practical enough and not simple enough.

Here's the key point. Almost anyone can write a novel. Writing a novel, of course, does not mean that it will get published and make you a lot of money. You already know how to write. You do it every day and have for a long time. Now it's only a matter of applying that writing experience to a different kind of project. Learning to begin a novel really isn't that difficult. I have taught novel writing for almost thirty years, both as a private writing consultant and college professor. I have worked with all kinds of people, of all ages, occupations, and backgrounds, and I have shown them *all* how to write and finish a novel. Many of them have been published, and a few have made a lot of money. Regardless, until you try, you won't know what will happen. You don't have anything to lose because the act of writing is itself a useful and enjoyable activity. Let's get started.

The first step is to come to some understanding about the novel writing process itself and to get rid of certain false presumptions or blocking ideas. Let's see if any of these quotations sound familiar to you.

"You can't really teach someone to write fiction."

This belief follows the old-school approach, and it is usually proposed by someone who has never dared to attempt to write creatively and who is therefore trying to discourage others from doing so. The pure fact remains that thousands of wonderful books are written and published every year, and all of the writers of these books have been taught to write. Obviously, even in the days before creative writing classes and workshops, and such books as this one, writers successfully completed novels. They must have learned somehow! What speakers of the above statement are really saying is that no one can teach them simply and directly. They resent the fact that they themselves gave up even before they started, and so they spread the lie that the writing process is some kind of gift from the gods, a mystical process reserved for a blessed few or for those willing to struggle through years of suffering. Nothing could be more wrong.

Everything a human being does is somehow learned, so it really comes down to how it is learned. It makes sense that if you can learn how to do something from someone who knows how to do it, it's better and faster than trying to learn it on your own. In fact, this principle is at the heart of the master-apprentice system which is the system that most artists and artisans have used for centuries in the training of others. In short, if you want to be a carpenter, you go to work for an experienced carpenter. Carpentry is a difficult trade, but it can be learned and mastered.

The same is true of writing fiction. You can learn the techniques, learn how to apply them, and write that novel you've always wanted to write.

"How-To-Write books are fine for formula writing, but they don't work if you want to write a _____ book."

Fill in the blank with any kind of novel you want to write, from a children's fantasy to a mainstream best seller. All types of novels have the same basic elements. No matter who your audience is; no matter how complex the story's conflict; no matter how experimental the techniques, all novels can be written by the system recommended in this book. In fact, you must never forget this one basic truth: a story *is* a story, no matter what else it is, and a story always has certain elements that make it what it is. When my daughter was little, I must have read her literally hundreds of stories, and I noticed that all of them had the same things in common. Typically, there was a bridge and a troll under the bridge and a small child afraid of trolls who had to cross the bridge to get what s/he wanted. *War and Peace*, a novel by Leo Tolstoy, has essentially the same ingredients; it is just a bit more involved and sophisticated.

The system in this book recognizes the essential aspects of writing a novel and shows you how to achieve them. Its approach is basic and simple, so that you can use it and also adapt it to any type of novel you want to write.

"The writing process is just too complex for the average person to master."

One of my writing teachers once told me a very wise thing, but it took me a long time to understand what he really meant. He said, "Remember that you can't think and write at the same time." Sounds a little absurd on the surface, doesn't it? Well, I finally discovered what he was implying. That the writing process (any kind of writing) is really made up of two overall things: (1) the activity of the human mind in thinking about *What to write*; (2) and the activity of the human mind in thinking about *How to write it*. We call these two activities content and technique. It makes sense when you think about it. Each of these two activities can be highly involving, and at times complex. It's a lot like trying to think about the techniques of playing basketball while playing in an actual game. Perhaps you have had the experience of trying to complete some kind of writing assignment in a hurry, coming up with what to say and at the same time phrasing it in words and sentences. You may remember how uncomfortable you felt, and perhaps how unsuccessful the final product was. The point is clear. Each of the two major activities is too compelling to allow one to distract from the other.

Writing is difficult for most people for one simple reason. They try to do too many things at once.

Any human process becomes more challenging than it really has to be when you try to cram together several of the natural steps in the process and perform them all at once. Remember the experience, perhaps at some gift-giving time, of putting something together? You had to follow a set of instructions in order to have a finished product . . . say a bicycle or maybe a barbecue set. You performed one simple act at a time until the bicycle or barbecue became the proud object of your efforts, almost before you realized it. The same system needs to be applied to the writing process, but seldom is. Somehow, most writing books that I've read seem to tell me how the completed "bicycle" or "barbecue" should look, but spend very little time telling me simply and specifically how to put them together. Most successful professional writers are not great geniuses. They're just like you and me. But they have been smart enough to learn one thing. They've developed a system which tells them what steps to take, when to take them, and especially *what the next step is*.

The writing of a novel can be achieved if you break the process down into simple, easily accomplishable steps, each step leading naturally to the next until the process is finished. Although this book is called *Beginning the Novel*, it is also designed to help you do something else. It's a fact that most novels never get done because they never get started correctly. If you follow the system within these pages, you will also finish your novel. Too good to be true? Try it and see.

And remember two things. First, that all creative accomplishments like the writing of a novel are best achieved when you realize that there needs to be a balance in your mind between what you plan in advance and what you discover as you go. *Intention* and *Discovery* are both important ingredients of this process, and they should be kept in balance. Go ahead and follow the system as it is outlined, but simultaneously don't be afraid to adapt your plan as the novel develops. In short, let your novel tell you what it wants to become.

And remember too that you're not alone in this endeavor. There's something else that will help you if you let it. Some people have called this entity "intuition" or "conscience." Writers call it "the Muse." But it really doesn't matter what you call it; all successful creative people know that it exists, and in fact, learn to rely upon it. Perhaps you've experienced the wonderful feeling that comes when you are involved in a successful and harmonious partnership. Things seem to get done faster and more productively. Well, you have a wonderful partner just waiting to help you, and believe it or not (and you must!), it is within your own psyche. You have probably already experienced its power during times which people call inspiration. Perhaps you have heard this voice of suggestion within your head, almost like someone whispering to you on the sly. And if you chose to follow its advice, you were probably benefitted by it. The more you realize that all successful creative projects are really best produced through such partnerships, the more at ease you will become and the more messages you will receive. Try not to let fear or doubt control you. Remind yourself that you are not creating this novel all by yourself. Literally, give yourself up to the power of patience and faith and believe that you will be given the necessary ideas and the skills to dramatize them. Your job is to be open enough and brave enough to accept this help.

It's also a good idea to record everything that comes to you, even at the oddest moments. Once you have committed yourself to the writing of your novel, all kinds of insights will arrive, generally "unbidden" and sometimes even "out of the blue." Of course, they are really not unbidden or out of the blue at all. They are actually a reflection of the more subtle workings of the human brain in partnership with the Force that created it.

Before going on in the book, read *The Great Gatsby* by F. Scott Fitzgerald. You can find an inexpensive copy in any book store, or a free one at your neighborhood library. I will be using examples from this book to illustrate my ideas, so you have to be familiar with it for the examples to be meaningful to you.

Task Summary:

Believe in the fact that you can write a novel and read *The Great Gatsby*.

William Faulkner was an obsessive binge drinker and probably an alcoholic.

STEP TWO

[The Techniques]

Task Procedure:

Learn about the fiction writing methods.

In order to write a novel, you need to know about the techniques of fiction writing, and in addition, how these techniques differ in some ways from those of other kinds of writing. All of you have written before; some of you have written fiction, perhaps even extensively. Regardless, all of you know that in order to create something challenging like a novel, you need to know something about the process itself. Many creative writing teachers are against making too many statements about how-to-write out of fear of stifling or inhibiting their students. Strangely enough, I have encountered just the opposite effect. Paradoxically, the more guidance I give to my students, the more free they feel to express themselves spontaneously. They are evidently not tied down by doubts and fears which stop them from writing. In one exciting way, the writing of a novel will involve you in a process of asking yourself many questions. And the answers to these questions will teach you to ask more questions, and these answers in turn will draw you more deeply into the process itself. A basic understanding of fiction writing techniques will give you the questions you need to ask. You will slowly gain the confidence necessary to learn "on the job" and at the same time, the incentive to finish what you have begun.

Language

The art of telling a story requires certain understandings

regarding what kinds of words work best and how different kinds of words achieve different responses from readers. Although no one can or should prescribe formulas for the word-choices you will make, there are some general effects that you need to know.

The nature of language in the most primitive sense is seldom appreciated because most of us have forgotten the moment when we were first exposed to words. When we were babies, words were just noise to us, and it was only later, as we grew, that we learned that language was noise of a special kind. "Language is sound, associated with an object or a concept and agreed upon." This basic definition is of interest to us novel-writers because it reminds us of the way readers will respond to the words we choose. Words are both arbitrary and conditioned in their eventual meanings and effects. Even though "barbed wire" is a phrase that probably means the same thing to everyone in a dictionary sense, it is also an image which will affect people very differently, depending on their association with it. Remember, that in one very basic way, people will react to your words as they have been conditioned to. Therefore, it's important for you to know in advance those characteristics of words that tend to significantly affect these reactions.

There is one primary difference between how most of us are trained to write (explanatorily) and how you now need to write (dramatically). All through your school and work years, you have been conditioned to send and receive words that serve the purpose of *informing*. When you write fiction, you now need to adopt your language usage to the needs of *dramatizing*. Simply put, you need to show, not tell. Therefore, certain style habits need to be changed in order to fit this new goal. But don't worry. With some practice, you can easily make this adjustment. In fact, one of the greatest poets of all time was Wallace Stevens. He was an insurance company executive who wrote poetry in his spare time. There are many successful writers with regular, full-time jobs who have learned the pleasures of writing as an avocation. James Dickey, a poet and the author of the novel *Deliverance*, was once asked to define a poet, and he said, "A poet is somebody who writes poetry." Well, you may have a regular job during the week, but at night or on weekends, you're a novelist.

Very few people will argue about the ultimate meanings of

words like *chair*, *car*, *building* and *book*, but wars, both private and public, may start with disagreements over words like *peace*, *democracy*, *civil rights* and *freedom*. The first group of words are called *concrete* words, the latter *abstract*. Both kinds are used in the writing of a novel, but each has a different effect on our readers. In general, concrete words make readers visualize the things which the words represent, and abstract words make readers think about them. The difference between "A raven sat at the top of an evergreen tree" and "An object of fear crowned the top of a thing of reverence" is profoundly great. No formulas can tell you when to use the various kinds of words, but it's useful to remember that, as a story teller, you are most often trying to make it possible for your readers to experience through their senses the things you are reporting.

Another characteristic of language you need to consider is its degree of *specificity*. "Several patrons of the establishment spent their time participating in physical actions," is essentially a concrete statement, but very general. Such words which cover many possible examples leave it to readers to "fill in" with specifics of their own. Sometimes that will be useful in a novel, but most of the time, especially in moments of immediate drama, you will want to encourage your readers to construct the actions in their own mind's eye, and you can best do that by describing everything in more specific words: "Four men in long black coats stood at opposite corners of the dim barroom heaving billiard balls at each other."

The goal of most non-fiction writing is to get across meaning directly, that is, by encouraging the reader to connect one sentence after another in a coherent flow of meaning. This process helps the reader think about what is being read. The goal of the novelist is different. You want your readers to participate in the story's events so that they can feel the emotion in the scenes which you are presenting. To encourage this participation in the emotional moments, you need to think of language as a medium, a means to an end more than an end onto itself, and use words that focus your readers on the things being described and not the words doing the describing. The poet Archibald MacLeish once wrote, "A poem should be wordless like a flock of geese." Now obviously, he wasn't actually suggesting a blank page, but merely pointing out that the less your readers are aware of the language and the more they are aware of what the language is creating, the more they will help contribute to the substance of the story you're writing. In this sense, you are really asking your reader to collaborate in the creation of the novel. It's what Thomas Hardy, the fine British novelist, called "the hidden content." It's a wonderful concept because it frees you the writer of having to "do it all" on your own. Your function in this partnership of writer-character-reader is to put down enough in the way of specific, concrete images to invite your readers to add to them. When you were watching a sad movie and started crying, someone might have rudely tapped you on the shoulder and asked you what was so sad about your life that you were crying while watching a movie. You would be partly justified in complaining to this person that it wasn't your life but the life of the character in the movie that was sad. Of course, both of you are right. Because you have experienced life enough to recognize the representation of certain sad events (or images!), you *add your emotions to those of the characters*, and thus you cry. You have literally helped create the drama. As writers of novels, you can easily tap into this hidden content by using the kind of words that best invite it.

All of you will write with what we call a different *style*. Style, generally defined, is the way we do something. It therefore involves many choices, some simple, some complex; some conscious and some unconscious. Regardless of the choices you make, try to become more aware of them and why you are making them, especially during the process of revision. And a final word about language. Remember that you now have a greater freedom to express yourself. There are no taboos about word usage to restrict you. Think of your words as a painter thinks of colors. Try to let your instincts fly free and allow your language the latitude to express what has perhaps been held back all of this time.

> Exercise:
> Pick a person whom you know very well and write a brief paragraph describing that person: 1) first in highly general and abstract words; 2) then in very specific and concrete words. You will get the feel of the different effects that

different words achieve and be more sensitive to their use in your novel.

Setting

Where your novel takes place will always comprise its most basic element, but not its most important. After all, your readers will be most interested in your characters and what they do. On the other hand, these characters will only become interesting if they are acting in a recognizable place and time. Of course, during the length of any novel, you will be describing many such places all of which are appropriate to the actions being performed. I can now bring up an important fictional term which applies to setting, as well as all other fictional techniques. It is called *materialization*. As I said earlier, your goal as a novelist is to help your readers see your characters and what is happening to them, so that they can grow to care about them and become involved in their lives. Writers call this attachment the "cheering factor." You are undoubtedly familiar with this element if you've ever been in a movie theater and heard the crowd (perhaps you among them!) cheer for some exciting event on the screen. Of course, in this movie, the viewers are getting a picture of the events automatically. As a writer, you have "only" words to achieve a series of ongoing images which your readers will construct in their own minds. The best way to accomplish this challenging task is to describe your settings in such vivid detail that they begin to *materialize* for your readers. Your readers in turn will come to believe in a very basic way that they are where you tell them they are, whether on a vast plain in the Soviet Union, the planet Venus or in a small Irish pub.

Setting is actually made up of several specific elements, each of which you can use to establish the necessary foundation for your story. Setting is, most basically, a composite of many specific places, most of which your readers will recognize even though they might never have experienced them firsthand. These places are called *physical backdrops*. They are similar to the stage settings used in the theater. In most cases, you should choose places with which you yourself are familiar. This procedure gives you an abundance of details from which to pick the necessary few, and also provides that almost magical emotional connection needed to help convince your readers of the reality of your story.

This emotional connection is called *sense of place*, and I will discuss it more fully a little later. Another, perhaps surprising ingredient of setting is *time*. Since a story is really a series of character actions, these actions inherently take up time and occur at some point in history. The connotations of time can be very helpful in establishing your readers' connection to the events you narrate. In most cases, these time elements will be a natural outgrowth of the other elements of setting. A third aspect of setting is perhaps even more surprising to you because, so far, I have been discussing inanimate or abstract things. All people in your novel who are not functioning as s (more on this later), should be considered as objects of setting and not human beings. Some of them may be very important to your novel (*antagonists*), but they really only exist in the story to make life complicated for your important character(s) (*protagonists*). Like avalanches or storms at sea, they are used as physical phenomena which force your major characters into situations of conflict. The best example of a setting character is the traditional villain who sets out to conquer the hero. If the villain did not exist, in one key sense, neither would the story.

Now that you're familiar with the elements of setting, you can understand how setting actually works in your novel. In fact, setting really has three different ways in which it helps you write your novel. First, it helps you establish *mood* or *atmosphere*. These are the emotional qualities of an environment that will inevitably create reader attachment. If a scene is described as sensual, gloomy or menacing, the foundation has been laid for the characters to perform appropriately. We are all familiar with how music establishes atmosphere in movies or television dramas. Once the cellos start playing, we know that something serious is about to occur. As a writer, you can use setting details to create this mood. A second function of setting is to provide for the plot. You will choose particular places which best suit the actions that you will need your characters to perform. You can also select settings which force your major character to face his/her antagonist(s). For instance, when you put a character into an unfamiliar and perhaps dangerous situation, you take away that person's normal way of reacting to life's dangers and create new and interesting tensions. In his short story, *An Outpost of Progress*, Joseph Conrad placed his two major characters in a

Belgian Congo jungle and gave them jobs to do for which they were not mentally or emotionally qualified. Their deterioration became evident, and when dramatized, helped create the story's plot. A final function of setting is to help you reveal what kind of characters you're writing about. Setting can aid in character creation in two ways: 1) characters, like you and me, choose what they want around them in terms of their own, personal surroundings, so that these choices in turn reveal something of what they are like; 2) characters who must face the challenges of a dangerous environment will also show how well or how poorly they are capable of doing so. This use of setting is one of the best ways to create drama for both a believable and intriguing conflict.

There is one final term that you need to know about, and it is really two terms in one. I referred to it earlier, and it's called *sense of place*. This is the emotional surge that you feel when you think of a certain time or place in your life. Perhaps it was a rustic cabin in the woods, a romantic picnic spot at the beach, or even a quietly rich moment at your kitchen table. In life, we all experience many such powerful moments and naturally come to associate them with the places where they occurred. You can exploit this common human experience by using such places in your novel. This connection will provide a detailed intensity which will come through your descriptions, because in the deepest sense of the word, you *know* what you're talking about. The great American poet Robert Frost once said, "No fire in the writer, no fire in the reader." You need to have a passionate knowledge of the settings you choose for your novel. Then sense of place will take on its second meaning, the same sense that you have, but transferred to your reader. We have all experienced the richness of reading a story which takes us out of our everyday world and transports us to a place created by the magic of words. Specific, deeply felt descriptions can achieve that magic if they are blended with other details of the story and are reflective of the particular character viewing the scene. In his short story, *The Princess,* D. H. Lawrence describes a certain mountain scene from the point of view of his major character, a young woman riding farther and farther away from safe civilization along side her attractive but dangerous guide. Lawrence more than gives us facts of physical geography; he gives us the state of mind and emotions which are registering these facts, thus making his readers, as it were, "become" his major character. The granite boulders are not just grey and rounded; they are brutish and rough. In your settings, look for details which will imply your characters' own impression of what is around them. That way, your readers will believe in your characters' existence and want to find out more about them.

> Exercise:
> Pick a specific place (indoors or outdoors) toward which you have a strong emotional connection. Tell your reader what happened there, trying to use as many details of Setting as you can to imply the atmosphere and also support the the action that occurred.

Plot

If you were to tell your friends that you were writing a novel, what would be their first question? What's it about? This is a natural question for anyone involved, even casually, in the story telling process. It's worth our time thinking about this question and what it really means. In the simplest sense, a story is a series of actions performed by people in certain locales. No matter how many fancy labels we may attach to these and other related elements, the elements themselves remain undeniable. These basic aspects help us because we know in advance what we have to do to create a novel. Still, in another sense, we have to "live up to" how *all* novels are written in achieving our particular version. And of all these basic elements, plot is the most necessary.

"The king died, and then the queen died" is a series of actions that seem related, but "The king died, and then the queen died of grief," is the beginning of a plot. E. M. Forster, the well-known British writer of such novels as *Howard's End* and *Passage to India*, thus speaks of this most basic of all fictional techniques, and goes on to explain the importance of causality in the telling of a story. What makes a plot and thus a novel interesting to readers are the emotional reasons for the actions which the characters perform. These emotional causes are what's behind the "innocent" question of "What's your story about?" Another way of asking the question might be, "What happens in your novel that might interest me?" As we all know, reading is hard work and always will be. We need to give our readers good reasons why they will spend their hard-earned money and time on reading your book. The agent and then publisher who will eventually sell your book will be looking for novels that have plots of emotional interest because they know what readers want.

Before we talk about how to create a plot for your novel, we need to discuss the nature of plot itself. Simply defined, plot is a series of actions performed by characters in a certain sequence. To make these actions interesting to readers, we need to incorporate three elemental things in our story: *mystery, suspense*, and *surprise (MSS)*. These are the three aspects which make life fascinating, and we need to build them into any plot we might construct.

Mystery is perhaps life's most intriguing force. Life itself is a mystery. Who are we? Where are we going? What is the ultimate meaning of our existence? These and other similar questions are monumentally important to people. There are, of course, mystery stories which particularly exploit this element, but in one very basic sense, all good stories are *mystery* stories. That is, on page one, we know nothing about the characters' lives and what they want, and as we turn the pages, we come to answer our initial questions and then realize that these answers only serve to create more questions. The story is able to thus draw us along, to compel us to keep reading it because it keeps creating little mysteries and solving them, while also fulfilling our larger curiosities about the characters' ultimate fates. Thus, mystery is created by our "not knowing" and resolved by our coming to know all we want to know.

Peculiar as it may sound, *suspense* is essentially the opposite. Suspense is created by our knowing about the characters to the extent that we want to read more about them (*sympathy*), but then coming to realize that these characters are somehow in danger. When characters want to achieve something, and in seeking it put themselves at risk, physically, mentally, emotionally or spiritually, the reader's interest is piqued. Thus as the story unfolds, more and more mystery is ended while simultaneously more and more suspense is created. We thus become ever more involved in the characters' problems and come to want to know the outcome of their destinies.

Surprise is not as important as the first two elements, but it can lend a pleasing effect to your novel by showing your readers that the story, like life itself, is filled with unforeseen events which impact importantly on the characters' success or failure. Such plot twists show the reader that your story is not predictable or mundane, and when these sudden turnabouts are based on real human motives and plausible actions, they become part of the pleasure of reading, of vicariously experiencing other peoples' lives.

In order to create mystery, suspense, and surprise in your plot, you need to think of your novel in terms of another basic element. When your characters' desires are somehow blocked or frustrated, tension is created in the story, and these tensions are called *conflict*. In turn, these conflicts are created by both external and internal causes. External conflicts are caused by characters other than the major character and sometimes by the forces of Nature itself. Internal conflicts are created by warring elements within the characters' hearts and minds. A male character may want to become a hero on the high seas, but is faced with jumping ship and deserting his passengers in order to save himself. Later, after having failed his duty, he learns that the ship did not sink and that, in fact, his career has already ended in disgrace. He must now face himself and choose what to do in reaction to his own cowardly action. What he accomplishes forms the brunt of Joseph Conrad's novel *Lord Jim*, and it is this combination of external and internal forces which literally create Conrad's novel. Sometimes, when all the tensions of a novel can be easily summed up, writers call this element the *central conflict*. Not all novels have a simplified central conflict, but it's a useful term to know, and I will come back to it in the early stages of your writing process.

Let's discuss two final concepts concerning plot, each of which will help you simplify the writing process. In his brilliant essay on creativity called *Poetics*, the Greek philosopher Aristotle wrote of a story's *structure*. It can sometimes be useful to step back and think of your novel in more general terms suggested by a certain pattern. For example, Aristotle thought of a story as having three main parts: a rising action, a climax, and a falling action. Many modern stories, especially on television or in the movies, do not fit comfortably into this familiar pattern, but many do. Rising action involves all those events in the first portion of the novel which create the conflicts mentioned above. The climax is that part of the story where the major character's conflicts are resolved, and falling action consists of any events that may follow that high point.

It can be equally useful to think of your characters' actions as representing one or more typical lifelike situations in which people have been involved since time immemorial. These situations are called *plot shapes* and are important in allowing you to think of your story in more simplified and therefore more universal terms. Some of the common plot shapes include: hunt, search, journey, combat, love triangle (and other angles!), reunion, survival, new kid in town, David and Goliath, loss and escape. As you can see, they represent primitive life situations which we can all relate to. No matter the surface trappings of time or space, your readers will understand the basic issues at stake in each of these situations and will become at least initially interested in the story which implies them. Obviously, not all stories fit easily into one of these categories (although some stories fit into more than one category simultaneously), but the concept itself can help you get started. It's like the wood frames that are put around wet cement during the construction of a new sidewalk. They are invaluable at first, but later unnecessary as the cement hardens. Such is the concept of plot shape. You can use it to start thinking about your story until later when your plot becomes formed more fully in your mind. Then you probably won't need it anymore. Try to be observant of life and add to the list of plot shapes given above by summing up the human situations which you encounter.

> Exercise:
> Pick one of the common plot shapes which you can remember experiencing, and describe its most climactic moment in simple, straight forward terms as if you were telling a friend about it. Remember, you will want to use as many details as you can, so that we can see what happened, and not just know about it. Examples might be a reunion with a very close friend/lover or a search for (and a finding) of something very important to you.

Character

If you were hired to sell a certain product door-to-door, you would spend your whole workday talking about that product, trying to sell it to your customers. You wouldn't spend hours talking about your new car or describing how to make a Caesar's salad. In a sense, your only justification for those hours during which you are earning your salary or commissions would be to represent the product company. Such a salesperson is the *major character* of a novel. He/She exists entirely to "sell" a product, in this case the plot. Both history books and novels talk about actions, but what makes the novel different from all histories is that it personalizes these actions through the intimate experience of a single person.

Thus, there is a crucial difference between art and life, that is between a character in a novel and the living person upon which that character was based. Characters in a novel are ultimately open to the reader. Their motives are eventually understood, and their actions consistent with those motives. People are never this way entirely. Characters in a novel can be trusted to always perform the same actions, no matter how many times you read the novel. Needless to say, people are not this trustworthy. Characters are simply defined so that there are no personality traits which do not directly apply to the actions they need to perform in the story. People are much more complex, and at no given moment will they act solely out of a singular, dramatic purpose. What I have been saying here is that art is coherent, permanent and unified, whereas life is contradictory, impermanent and chaotic.

In order to "represent" the plot, and more specifically the major conflicts, a major character must be thought of as an (art)tificial construction which creates the illusion that he/she is a real person. The major character walks, talks and thinks like you and me, but does these things with only one question in mind. Do they serve the story? In addition, as I said earlier, the major character is different from all other "characters" in your novel. Other characters should be thought of as objects which are used to help create the major tensions in the story. They do not exist (like the major character) to make the ultimate choices and live or die by those choices. They are there to force the major character to choose. Therefore, the major character is generally more complex than the other characters. He or she will have different, and sometimes contrasting, personality traits. The major character is also capable of surprising the reader and thereby engaging the reader's interest and sympathy.

Just as you get to know the people in your life, you will (with one exception) have your readers come to know your major character(s). The ways in which human beings become acquainted are of two types, and they are called *external* and *internal methods of characterization*. This term may sound complicated, but the process is really very simple. When you meet other people for the first time, you learn about them by how they look, what they say and do and how they deal with the places which they have chosen as their surroundings. The exception I mentioned earlier, which is not available to us as living creatures, is a presentation of what the other person is feeling or thinking. They can tell us about these things, but we won't know for sure if they're communicating the complete truth of what's actually in their minds.

The so-called external methods of major characterization are *physical appearance*, *dialogue*, *actions*, and *setting*. First, we have already discussed how setting can help you reveal your major characters by the environments they choose and the success or failure they achieve in facing possible challenges from those environments. Next, there is a basic fact about physical appearance which you can exploit as a fiction writer. It's probably true to a great degree that what people look like will affect what they do, and in turn, what they do will determine what they look like. So when you describe your major characters' outward appearances, you help your readers see them and become convinced of their actuality. Dialogue is also a major aspect of any story, and it is rich with implications of major character. What your major characters say and how they say it will imply much about them. Obviously, most important is what your characters do and don't do when faced with the conflicts you create for them. Their actions are the most potent revealers of what they're really like, and will therefore be the most dramatically interesting evidence of your story's meaning.

The internal methods of characterization are called *exposition* and *stream of consciousness*. Since the development of a more formal awareness of human psychology, writers have become fascinated with showing what their characters are thinking. In fact, it is the one big advantage fiction has over the movie or play. It is a very powerful technique and should not be over-used, but a judicious revelation of what your characters are thinking can add greatly to your readers' understanding of them. When employing exposition, you will use words like "thought," "wondered," "mused" and so forth. If you want to reveal your characters' thoughts directly from their own minds without using these words, you will be using stream of consciousness. This latter term was coined by James Joyce and attempts to represent the chaotic state of a person's mind. Of course, ultimately the presentation must not be chaotic, but only appear to be. It is actually quite planned and hopefully clarifying. The latter method is still considered experimental and is quite complex in its makeup and application, so unless you are an experienced writer, it will probably be best for you to use exposition, at least at the beginning of your writing career.

Remember that the reader will be interested in your story if you present interesting characters in your novel. Spend time thinking about these people and discover what it is about them that makes them emotionally interesting. Then apply that knowledge to the prescriptive steps that come later in this book.

> Exercise:
> Select a person very close to you (perhaps yourself!) and pick a time and a place where you/we would normally encounter that person. Then pretend that you are describing that moment for someone who does not know this person. Try to give as full a picture as you can, using both the external and internal methods of characterization.

Point of View

Thousands of years ago, story tellers did not write down their stories. Early earth dwellers often told stories in pictures carved in stone or on walls. Certainly, people recalled and elaborated upon their experiences verbally, but there was no group called "fiction writers." Even up to modern times, the reproduction of the written word was a painstaking and time consuming task. Stories were often told by wandering minstrels with accompaniment of music. These people were called troubadours, and they sang ballads with commonly-known characters and plots. Due to the nature of the medium and their audience, they had to keep their stories simple and accessible. In time, the staged drama became popular and stories were presented by actors in a church or on a especially constructed stage, sometimes outdoors or sometimes in what came to be called a theater.

With the invention of the printing press, stories could finally be written down and produced somewhat less arduously, but even as late as the nineteenth century, books as we know them were not a common commodity. Writers had to first prove themselves to be popular by reaching audiences of various magazines or periodicals. Novelists had to write in brief, interesting episodes to please the monthly subscribers. Only after they gained some success were they allowed to publish their stories in books. Even so, the form of the story maintained its long conditioned habit in recognizing the existence of the writer-audience relationship. Writers like Henry Fielding and Samuel Richardson, and later Charles Dickens and William Thackeray, continued to address their readers within the pages of their novels. This method, in fact, eventually became known as the "dear-reader" approach.

From the perspective of the story teller, this arrangement was perhaps not always pleasing because no matter how skilled the writers were, the readers would always to some extent be aware of the writers' presence. But with the arrival of *realism* as a popular concept in the arts, writers realized that a sense of their own presence in the story took away from the readers' ability to participate intimately in the lives of the characters. In other words, novelists began to give more weight to the characters' versions of what was happening in a story, and less to their own, more complete and more powerful versions. Authors like de Stendhal (*The Red and the Black*), Gustave Flaubert (*Madame Bovary*), Nathaniel Hawthorne (*The Scarlet Letter*), and Mark Twain (*Huckleberry Finn*), were only a few of the many writers who were beginning to apply the new "realistic" techniques. In order to convince readers that they were experiencing real, everyday life in all of its actuality, realistic authors attempted to have their own voice disappear, so that readers would instead hear the thoughts and feelings of the characters without any authorial interference. When writers chose their characters and not themselves to tell their stories, *point of view* was born.

Point of view is really very simple. It is defined as the character or characters through whom the story is rendered. Because fiction writers do not present their characters' actions directly to an audience as playwrights do, they must choose various ways of referring to the characters in the story. As you know, there are only three ways of referring to someone in the English language other than by a proper name. This form of reference is called *person*, and our only singular choices are: first (I), second (you), and third (he, she, it). Of course, the plural versions are: first (we), second (still you), and third (they). These are the available alternatives in referencing a character. When you refer to your characters' speech, thoughts or actions in your novel, you will use one of these persons . . . or points of view. They are more well known as first-person, second-person, and third-person points of view. As the example below shows, each point of view choice will create a different relationship between your readers and your characters.

> I watched her from across the room. (first-person)
> You watched her from across the room. (second-person)
> He/She watched her from across the room. (third-person)

Notice how both the first- and third-person versions establish a character-based perspective, but how the second-person version, at least potentially, directs the reader's attention to someone other than a character in the story. The "you" addressed might just be the reader, and therefore the presence of the writer is emphasized, destroying the basic purpose of point of view. Thus, second-person point of view is seldom used, except in rare and momentary instances.

Your choice of point of view will be important because no matter which one you pick, you will have a different story. I first discovered this fact in one of my own early writing experiences. I had written a short story but didn't like the third-person point of view which I had selected. So, being young, inexperienced and lazy, I merely went through the story and changed all the pronouns to "I" and of course made the verbs agree. My astute friend kindly volunteered to read the story, and afterward he responded by saying, "You know, I really like this story, except that there's something strange about it. For the life of me, I know it's written in first-person, but it really sounds like it's written in third." Thus, I learned that changing the point of view really makes all the difference in the world in the setting, plot and character details you choose. Another way of saying it is—perspective is everything. So, when the time comes, study the factors presented later in the book, and make your best choice. You may change it later, but by then you will know why you are doing so, and you will also know to re-write those old portions of the novel and not merely change the pronouns!

> Exercise:
> Pick a common moment from your own life in which there are at least two people. Examples might be a shopping trip or an athletic endeavor. Choose one of the participants and briefly tell your readers about this event. Then choose the other person and repeat the process. Study the differences in the way you had to change your words.

> **Task Summary:**
>
> > **Practice working with the methods of Setting, Plot, Character and Point of View by repeating each of the exercises several times.**

Ernest Hemingway's father committed suicide, as did Hemingway himself.

STEP THREE

[The Idea]

Task Procedure:

Create an idea for your novel.

The only thing this book can't give you is an idea for your novel, but it can help you find it on your own. No matter who you are or what you've done, you've lived a life worth writing about. Too many times I've heard people say, "Oh, I can't write a novel. I haven't lived!" By that statement, of course, they mean that they haven't done things like going over Niagara Falls in a barrel or traveling around the world in a hot-air balloon. I have news for you. Neither have most of the successful writers out there. All of you have already lived a lifetime full of stories. It's only a matter of discovering those elements which will interest others. Emily Dickinson, one of America's greatest writers, left her small New England hometown only once in her life and never married. It is a matter of realizing that every life, your life, is universal and filled with meaningful events. You can also research people, places and things which you don't yet know about and create worlds which you haven't actually experienced first hand.

You've read this far in the book because somewhere down deep you actually believe in your own worth. This faith is important. My mentor once said, "Writing is an aggressive act!" He meant that people who have the courage and energy to express themselves to others (no matter in what form or how skillfully) are really demonstrating the importance of their own individuality by not being content to let the world pass them by unnoticed.

In order to gain the necessary confidence to write a book, you must be convinced that what you are going to write about is worth the effort. I don't think it's a good idea to write a novel with the sole motive of making money, or becoming famous. There should be something about the process itself which you enjoy. I have noticed that highly successful performers and athletes are successful in large measure because they become "taken up" by their own immediate participation. So to gain this wonderful, personal connection with your own efforts, you need to think of a starting point. There are many different places for the idea of a novel to be planted and become germinated. I deliberately use garden terminologies because the creative process in you has much in common with the growth process in Nature. A tomato plant must start from a seed, grow to a seedling and then to a fully mature plant. It needs time to accept the nurturing encouragement of sun and water, and then it needs more time (and patience from the grower!) for the tomatoes to form and eventually ripen. We need to think of ourselves as plants in Nature who must go through each step in the creative growth process in order to obtain the maturity of our own achievement. We must also perform each of these steps as fully as possible. This process takes patience, and also faith. We need to believe that because of our own efforts, we will receive the insights we need in order to write our novel. Give yourself time to think of ideas, and when they come, write them down. These valuable suggestions may not come again!

Character is the most natural element to begin with. Perhaps you know an interesting person whose life you would love to write about. You cannot write a complete biography of this person in a novel, but you can capture the basic elements that make this person unusual. Plot is also a fruitful starting point. Maybe you were involved in an interesting life situation. Although perhaps not headline news, the situation demonstrated some significant truths about life or presented an exciting and suspenseful challenge to you and others involved. Maybe somebody you know or read about performed an unusually unique action which captured your imagination. This single act could be expanded into a meaningful plot. Finally, there might be places in your life where something important happened to you. When you think about these places, you get a strong emotional charge. Although setting is seldom the exact starting point for a story, it can begin the suggestive chain reaction of feelings that will take you to character and plot.

Most writers, of course, begin with themselves as the major character, the actions of their own lives as plot and their own familiar environments as setting. If you have the objectivity to "get outside" of yourself, these are probably the best places to start. Regardless of where you start, you will need to have a full and honest understanding of your own personal emotions. What makes you happy, angry, excited, passionate, sad? You will evoke these emotions via the actions of your characters. Even in the most cold-blooded adventure novel, this emotional connection with your characters will help you persevere through the long, sometimes difficult hours of writing a book. Each day that you go to write, you will feel again the emotions that made you start your story in the first place. You will look forward to returning to this fictional world which is forming before your eyes.

So, in order to gain the necessary emotional insights to begin your novel, you need to focus on typical human actions and the elemental and sometimes primitive causes behind them. All of us are basically the same when it comes to the emotional reasons for why we do what we do, and I call these reasons *motifs*. All people feel these emotions. Taken together, they are mainly what makes us human. They are, therefore, what makes a story interesting because they cause conflicts. Some of the motifs which dominate the human condition are:

> love (in all of its many forms)
> fear
> hate
> sexual desire
> anger
> desire (other than for love/sex)
> revenge
> jealousy
> greed
> envy
> pride
> remorse
> guilt

When a specific motif is tied to a particular character in one moment of time, it becomes the character's *motive*. In most cases, these motives are universal and well understood by your readers even before they start reading your book. They are powerful forces for drama because the actions which your characters will perform from these motives are automatically understood and therefore interesting. And finally, when these emotionally based actions become important enough to take on a recognizable dimension, they form plot shapes. As I mentioned earlier, these plot shapes are those primary life events which have occurred since time began. They have automatic appeal because most people have experienced them in one form or another. As an example, let's take the novel which I asked you to read, *The Great Gatsby*, by F. Scott Fitzgerald.

The major character Jay Gatsby has a love/sexual desire *(motif)* for a former girl friend whom he lost when he was young. Now older and wealthy, he arranges his life to find and win back this girl, Daisy Buchanan *(motive and search)*.

Once you have established the initial motif(s) and motive(s) which lead to the awareness of a plot shape, you may find that they suggest additional ones. For instance, in *The Great Gatsby*, it happens that Daisy is already married when Gatsby finally finds her, so that a kind of *love triangle* is formed, within which Gatsby and the husband Tom Buchanan wage an under-the-surface *combat* for the hand of Daisy. In fact, Tom Buchanan's greed and jealousy become major factors in forming the climax of the novel.

Of course, not all novels fit comfortably into the above formula. *Catcher In the Rye* by J. D. Salinger is one such novel which defies categorization. But most novels can be thought of in the above terms, and certainly, if you are a writer of lesser experience, you have nothing to lose by applying the principle.

Taken together, the motif(s), motive(s), and plot shape(s) form what writers call the *premise* of a novel. The premise is usually a brief, three or four sentence summary of the novel's central problem. An expanded version of the premise will eventually become what is called the *central conflict* (CC). Both the premise and the central conflict are of course oversimplified, but this simplicity is what you need in the beginning. The premise is like the seed of a plant. Later it will naturally be surpassed by the plant itself, but in the beginning, it is all important. It is important to note that the premise *doesn't have to work from an awareness of specific characters.* You should be able to summarize your premise apart from mentioning individual people and their particular traits. For example, the general premise of *The Great Gatsby* would be a situation in which an older person is obsessed with recovering something from his/her younger days and is blinded by the impossibility and thus the destructiveness of doing so. This blindness makes the person vulnerable to the forces of the world which are always there to insure a negative ending. Notice that this premise could be used to tell the story of many different kinds of people in almost any age of human history, but it is precisely this situation which forms the necessary foundation for any story worth telling. Once your premise is in place, you can go on to brainstorm all the tension elements which have so far been suggested. Tension elements are those specific aspects of the story which cause complication for the major character and potentially harm or block the major character. You can divide these tension elements into three categories, those elements of plot mentioned earlier: mystery, suspense and surprise. Keep a running list of these three elements. They will act to suggest new insights, as well as to keep in order those already listed. You have now reached the end of the first stage in the process.

Task Procedure:

Develop your novel's idea through the following process:

1. Starting Points (People, Situations, Places)
2. Motifs (Basic Human Emotions Tied to a Major Character)
3. Motives (Specific Emotions Tied to this Character)
4. Plot Shapes (Basic Life Situation[s] Dramatizing #3)
5. Premise (General Statement(s) of #2, 3 and 4)
6. Tension Elements (Mystery, Suspense and Surprise)

It is best to follow the procedure in the way it is laid out, but since the human mind seldom works in an entirely orderly way, you should be alert for continuous suggestions that will make you go back and forth within the process itself while, at the same time, slowly moving forward.

Note: At the end of each step, I will give a brief example of what Fitzgerald *might* have written if he had followed this process in the writing of *The Great Gatsby*.

1. Starting Points: find yourself a comfortable place to sit which is free of distraction and then brainstorm the following:

a) People: name and briefly describe those people in your life who you think might be interesting enough to be major characters in a novel (remember to include yourself!). This step, like those below, will probably take more than one sitting. You will be constantly adding to your list as you go through your days, but the important point is that you have told your mind what you need, and now your mind (like the good computer that it is) will begin the work of scanning itself for useful material. A good way to prompt this and the other lists is to work through your life chronologically, starting from your earliest memories and working your way to the present day. You will find that this kind of contemplation will not only provide an enjoyable and useful way to begin the planning process, but will also pay great dividends in the form of continued discoveries during the actual writing itself.

b) Situations: name and briefly describe those events in your life which you would call memorable. These don't have to be hugely significant events to anyone else. They are events which excite you when you think about them.

c) Places: name and briefly describe those places in your life which you remember with a powerfully emotional connection. In fact, this emotional connection may not have any absolute relationship to what happened there or who was there at the time. Perhaps it is just something about the magic of the place (good, bad, or both) that captures your imagination.

Example:
As a starting point, Fitzgerald probably knew somebody (or many somebodies!) like Jay Gatsby. Everything we know about the author tells us that

he was fascinated with wealth and all of its ramifications. Add to this fascination for the rich and the powerful, Fitzgerald's decided bent for nostalgia and what-might-have-been, and he had all the makings of a plot seed. Tie power and license to this tendency to live in the past, and then make the most important part of that past a lost love, and he had his starting point.

2. Motifs: take your starting point and list all the human emotions which you feel are associated with it. Then begin to think of these emotions as present in a specific human being or major character.

Example:
At this point, Fitzgerald would have probably personalized the above general situation by choosing a single protagonist. He would have made this man very, very rich, perhaps through illicit means, in order to give him a shadowy background and make him all the more romantic. For his major character, he could have created a composite of many men of his acquaintance, including himself. But to make this character live in the past to a destructive sense, the character would have to want something very badly, something that was unattainable and also dangerous to him. What other motif was there at this point except love/sex?

3. Motives: now take the emotions which you have listed and tied to a major character and begin to specify the nature and personality of the major character. You will especially focus on this character's special reasons for acting as he/she does, probably coming up with additional emotions which will propel the budding plot. The exact nature of the major character's desires will also begin to take shape, as will some idea of what will stop him/her from gaining it (at least until the end).

Example:
Here is where Jay Gatsby began to take shape as

a full-blown character. It was probable that Fitzgerald discovered his need for a narrator later in the writing process, so Nick Carraway would have to wait his turn to be born. But it was also probable that Daisy Buchanan was fast appearing on the stage in the author's mind. Daisy was, in fact, much like Fitzgerald's own wife, Zelda, both in personality and background. The difference between art and life here was that Fitzgerald managed to win the love of his life, and Gatsby didn't. Of course, of such catastrophes are novels made. So now he had a major character who had made himself rich and powerful in order to "qualify" for the love of a woman whom he'd lost as a young man. Gatsby's obsession to find her, no matter how long it takes or whom it hurts, becomes the driving motive of the plot. This motive becomes *desire* for what he could have had, and the plot shape begins to mature into the plot itself.

4. Plot Shape: at this point, you will probably know (as Fitzgerald did) what the basic plot shape(s) will be. Others will suggest themselves as needed, but the initial shape is useful in providing boundaries of thought, within which you can begin to invent more specific aspects like other minor characters (including the antagonist[s]), other action-situations and settings. Try to keep your planning simple at this stage, but of course write down all suggestions that come to you. The unity which comes with the realization of your overall action pattern will give you confidence that you are working with story elements of universal appeal. These should excite you enough to go on with the hard work of developing your novel.

Example:
Obviously by now, the author realized that his major character was on a secret but desperate *search* for Daisy Buchanan. His thinking would now turn to the specific people and places that he (Gatsby) would need to accomplish his quest.

It was perhaps now that Fitzgerald also discovered that he couldn't have Gatsby tell his own story and that he would need someone else, perhaps a narrator who would help Gatsby achieve his dream. At any rate, he would place Gatsby in a mansion which would be vulnerable to visitors in the hopes that his love might one day wander in uninvited. And, of course, it was also at this point that the author found the one important early piece of his story, the fact that Daisy was married and had a husband who would not only be very much different from Gatsby, but who would also be his enemy. Thus, the *love triangle* and *combat* shapes were added, and together with *search*, they formed the working Premise.

5. Premise: now you will be able to tell yourself what your novel is about in the simplest, yet most dramatic, terms. Take those plot shapes which have been suggested and tied to a major character and state them in a sentence or two, highlighting those elements which produce the greatest emotional tension. You will eventually expand this portion of your planning to include a growing cast of minor or catalytic characters needed to create the central conflict. Elements of setting will also present themselves as appropriate to the characters and their actions. After you have written your premise, it should excite you to go on because it is both dramatically interesting and plausible. From this step forward, you will have to be true to it, or modify it so as to suit your growing discoveries.

Example:
I have already presented the simple form of Fitzgerald's premise for *The Great Gatsby*. At this point, the author was probably discovering the need for a growing cast of characters to occupy Gatsby's world and to function as complications in the Plot. Perhaps the author was also beginning to fill out his original concept of Nick Carraway, the first-person narrator,

realizing that this character would have to play a more important role than mere witness. In assembling a cast of characters to make the plot come alive, Fitzgerald most likely realized that he had to set up a series of checks and balances in tension, placing Daisy at the center of Gatsby's obsession and surrounding her with characters who would complicate Gatsby's attempts at winning her for his own.

6. Tension Elements (mystery, suspense and surprise): it is now necessary to begin the process of refining your plot, of making and remaking those specific choices which will end up as actual ingredients of your novel. Make three separate lists with the above headings, and include all the elements of each one that you can think of. These aspects will serve you in two major ways:

a) as specific things you will need to dramatize;
b) as suggestive vehicles of other things you will need in building an intricate and causally related plot.

For now, however, just put these elements down without thinking about them too much. In some cases, you may have only a few items on each list, and in terms of surprise, you may have none. Don't worry. You are in the beginning phase of invention and are building the foundation for future discoveries which will in turn fill out these lists.

Example:
Under mystery, Fitzgerald could have listed such items as: Daisy's whereabouts; Gatsby's background; their early life together; Gatsby's intentions in finding Daisy; Daisy's reactions if found; Daisy's husband's reactions; the success or failure of Gatsby's obsession. Under suspense, he obviously would have listed many of the same elements, but added: Daisy's ultimate choice of men; Gatsby's ultimate actions in response to this choice; the emotional and physical risks Gatsby

was taking in seeking to take another man's wife, i.e., Tom Buchanan's reactions. Under surprise, at this point, Fitzgerald probably could list nothing, but he obviously was starting to think of the outcome of his story and what it would bring in terms of unforeseen twists. Once he had decided Daisy's choice and shown what kind of man Tom was, his ending was probably becoming inevitable. Both Fitzgerald and Tom Buchanan knew that Gatsby wasn't the kind of man to take "no" for an answer, at least as long as he was alive. It was doubtful that, at this point, the author had worked out the exact surprise element of the final catastrophe. He only knew that he would need something to make the climax all the more poignant and ironic.

You have now come to the end of this stage in the planning process. It is a good idea to let these elements ripen in your consciousness for some time before going on to the next step. Time is the great teacher. It will show you how far you have come, and also how far you have to go. With the help of this book, renew your faith in yourself and your growing enterprise. You will be given the necessary information and insights with which to go forward.

Task Summary:

Create your novel's Premise.

Thomas Wolfe could not bring himself to organize his writing, so Maxwell Perkins did it for him.

STEP FOUR

[The Characters]

Task Procedure:

    Develop major and minor Characters for your novel.

    Now that you have a good start on your story, it is time to focus more intimately on your major and minor characters. At this point, the plot is taking shape and telling you what you will need in terms of people who will perform the necessary actions. When you began your lists of mystery, suspense and surprise elements, you most likely included several people. Let's remember that we need at least one major character to respond to the important events of the novel and several minor ones to help create these events. But also remind yourself that you need *only* those characters who are absolutely necessary to the creation of this conflict. For example, just because biographical fact or typicality dictates that most families have children, your fictional family should not have children unless they serve to make the conflict more complex and thus more interesting. Whether you are basing your novel's characters on real people (including yourself) or composites of real people, you need to stop thinking of these people as living and breathing folks and start thinking of them as fictional vehicles, necessary to the art of the novel. You will make your choices of characters and character traits on the basis of their appropriateness to the story's plot. Aspects of human psychology can be very useful in suggesting possible plot actions, but always remember that story itself takes precedence. In my class, I use the analogy of a sculptor starting with a shape of some kind, say a horse. The artist uses wire to form the rough outline of the horse's body (plot), and then takes a substance like paper or plaster of Paris (character) and puts it around the wire form to finally create the familiar image of the horse. It is the wire form (plot) that tells the artist where the substance (character) goes, not vice versa. It is true that character will eventually be the most important part of your novel, but your readers will not be interested in your characters unless they are involved in an interesting story.

Writers will argue over which of these elements is primary (the old chicken or the egg debacle perhaps), but there is little dispute over what is the most enjoyable part of writing a novel. As a writer, you are like a god when you are creating your fictional characters. But it is this intoxicating power that can also be your worst enemy. You need to adopt a respect for your characters, so that you will listen to them and follow their lead in what they want to do in your story. Yes, it is *your* story in the beginning, but it will become *their* story eventually, and the wise writer is he/she who lets the characters have free reign in the early drafts. A vital and viable character involved in a conflict situation will often "discover" new and intriguing actions which you the writer did not intend. All successful professionals know what it feels like to yield to a powerful character and see that character create nuances of the story that they could never have conceived beforehand. If it's any consolation, you can always go back later and change things to suit your own will, but I wouldn't recommend that you make these changes until you have fully realized the value of what your characters have taught you about your story.

Obviously, being the writer of a novel involves you in a partnership with your characters. You will create a working partnership with your characters (especially your protagonist[s]) in order to involve them in a relationship with your readers. You don't ever want to trick a character or unfairly deceive a reader. You will, of course, withhold information about your characters when it is artistically justified (more on this later), but you must work hard to gain the reader's trust that your characters have a mind and heart of their own and that they can be relied upon to perform according to the criteria which you have established for them. In order to suspend their disbelief and become involved in your story, your readers will need to see your characters materialize consistently, but not arbitrarily. Therefore, it is useful for you the "creator" to act with a humble heart and mind in your conception of character and wait with patience and faith for your characters to take you along for the ride. It is your job to create the story for them. Once you've done that, and picked the necessary people to make the story come alive, follow your characters' lead in the discovery of appropriate actions, especially in the early stages of writing. Later, you can stand some distance away from them and observe whether their decisions have been good ones and whether they do indeed service the needs of the plot as you conceived of it. And all along, of course, you will be creating this working relationship with your characters with the motive of inviting your readers to become your characters and participate in their story. To accomplish this reader involvement, you will need to first provide an incentive for them to care about your characters and then allow them to add their own personal knowledge of life so that they can identify with your characters and literally "become them." In this identification, the readers are helping you "write" your novel.

Major Character

Even though you have probably by now chosen your major character(s), remember that this choice isn't necessarily permanent. Once you get into the writing of your novel, you may discover that you've chosen the wrong person(s), and you will have to change your mind. Regardless, when you are working with a major character, ask yourself five simple questions as a means of testing whether your major character will be able to function effectively to register the central conflict (premise) which you have chosen. The questions are:

1. What does my major character want?
2. What stops him/her from getting it?
3. What does he/she do to remove this block?
4. Does the major character get what he/she wants?
5. Why or why not?

"Simplify, simplify," Pablo Picasso said. This famous artist did not mean to make things simple in the sense of making them uncomplicated or childish. He meant that artists of all kinds need to get to the essential core of a particular creative process or experience, to become acquainted with its most elemental and therefore its truest parts. Only by an absolute knowledge of each part of a motor—what it is made of and how it works—would we become a master of motor craft. To take apart the fictional engine and see it in its actual, "simplest" context—this is the task that the writer must perform. So the asking of the above questions cuts through the alleged complexities of human motives and informs us regarding what our story is really about. In one sense, all great stories are essentially simple stories. And the paradox insists that, indeed, if they are not at first simple stories, their complexities will never make them great.

Task Procedure:

Write a detailed autobiography of your major Character.

To deepen your early concepts of your major character and to help answer the above questions, your next task is to write a detailed autobiography of your major character(s). Take your major character from birth and have him/her speak to you in his/her own words in the first-person voice. Your major character should tell you everything that can be recalled in as much detail as s/he can manage, even down to specific moments or scenes that were important in his/her life. Obviously, you should rely as much as possible on actual biographical facts, but do not be afraid to invent facts and feelings which come to you as you are writing the autobiography. Two important things will be achieved by a patient and thorough effort at this stage of the planning process. You will come to know your major character very well, and you will also begin to think of him/her as a character in a novel and not a living person. It's probable that you will in fact know more about your major character than you'll actually need to, but because of this depth of knowledge, you will more skillfully dramatize your character once the story begins. One final suggestion: stop writing the biography at the point in the major character's life where the novel begins. An entirely different inventive process will take hold once the character starts to live in the first pages of your story.

The following are some of the aspects of a person's life which can be used as a brainstorming mechanism while your major character is writing his/her autobiography. This list can be looked at as a handy prompter of typical information, but it should not be regarded as a limiting device. There will be many items in your character's life which will not come under any of the following headings:

Physiology:
    Name
    Age
    Height and weight
    Coloring of hair, eyes, skin
    Unusual features
    Posture
    Appearance
        to the person him/herself
        to others
    Shape of head, face, limbs, body
    Grooming of self, clothing
    Defects
        deformities
        health
        abnormalities
        birthmarks
        in speech, sight, hearing
    Heredity
        paternal
        maternal
Sociology:
    Class
    Occupation
    Type of work
        duties
        income
        conditions
        attitudes toward work, employer
    Suitability for work
    Education
        elementary
            kind of school
            grades
            favorite subjects
            poorest subjects

      extra curricular activities
      aptitudes
   high school
      same as above
   college
      same as above
Home Life
   background (genealogy)
      maternal
      paternal
   parents
      attitude toward major character
      attitude toward each other
      relationship with
      marital status
      prevailing home atmosphere
      social strata
      social development
      mental development
      acquaintances
      habits (vices and virtues)
   own home life
      marital status
      children
      all the above
Service record
Religion
Race and nationality
Place in community
   organizations
   political connections
Amusements and Hobbies
   physical activities
   cultural activities
      reading
      the arts
Criminal Record,
   cause
   seriousness
   effects on life

Psychology:
    Sex life
    Moral standards
    Ambitions
    Frustrations
    Conflicts
    Temperament
    Attitudes and Values
    Complexes
        fears
        obsessions
        inhibitions
        superstitions
        manias

During the writing process, many different items will come to you that do not fit under any particular category. Write them down anyway. Each item that you write will add to your growing certainty that this character is as real or more real than anyone you know in life. What you will want to center on eventually are those aspects of the character's personality and background that helped produce the conflict situation which the character is facing at the start of the novel. You might not show this background in the novel itself, but your understanding of it will act as a force behind every action this character performs and make it convincing to your readers.

Minor Characters

As I mentioned earlier, all other characters in your novel should be thought of as catalysts, entities that look like people, talk like people and even think like people, but who actually function the same as a driving rain storm or an avalanche. These latter forces make people react to them, and that's the way you will want your minor characters to function. These characters are not minor in importance to your story, but they do not change once they are established, and they do not (as the major character does) make the important decisions in meeting the challenges of the central conflict.

The most important of these characters are the antagonists, characters who are the primary creators of the overall problem for the major character. These characters may be wonderful people or horrible people, but they all have one thing in common—the creation of tension/conflict for the major character. In Lawrence's *Lady Chatterley's Lover*, the antagonist is the gamekeeper Mellors. Because she falls in love with Mellors, the protagonist Constance Chatterley must now face a difficult choice: does she follow her heart and choose to live with the man she loves, or should she follow her conscience and stay with the impotent and materialistic Clifford Chatterley who happens to be her husband? Mellors and Chatterley are obviously crucial characters in Lawrence's novel, but they are not the person who faces this dilemma and thus are not the character through whom most readers will experience the story. Such minor characters must be complex up to a point and no further. Avoid making your minor characters so complex that your readers will become more interested in them than the major character. Usually, this switch of allegiance will not happen, if you remember to focus every character choice on the major character's central conflict.

Once you have chosen those minor characters who are absolutely essential to the early development of the plot, other characters might suggest themselves as the process continues. You may find yourself eliminating early choices, adding others, and even blending the activities of several previously chosen characters into a single character. This kind of "character economy" will add force to your novel and make the writing process more concise and powerful. In general, you will want to keep your cast as small as possible, thus enabling you to make even the most minor of characters interesting to your readers in significant ways.

To make your minor characters interesting, conceive of them as having agendas or concerns of their own, some of which will perhaps clash with the major character's and also contrast with other minor characters. For example, you will not want to show two sisters who each have the same basic personality and thus who each create the same effect on the major character. If you will need both of them, they should be portrayed as contrasting in some important way, so that they will create a different dynamic in the scenes in which they appear. Perhaps one sister is intent on getting a date with the major character, and the other is trying to avoid him. Or perhaps the first is essentially a selfish extrovert, and the second a shy, reclusive woman. Remember, however, to avoid making the minor character's wants and desires so powerful that they overcome those of the major character. In William Shakespeare's play *Othello*,

Iago, the antagonist, has been overlooked for promotion and vows to take revenge on the major or title character. He plots to make Othello jealous of his wife's alleged attentions for another man. From this point on, the author concentrates on Iago only in so far as he is the perpetrator of the conflict, and dramatizes with much greater complexity the reactions of Othello who is facing the challenges inherent in the conflict. Shakespeare does not go deeply into Iago's life or personality but keeps him acting from an easily understood motive, so that he can probe the depths of his major character's psyche as he (Othello) succumbs to the evil antagonist. As you are reading a novel or watching a movie, stop to analyze how the major character and minor characters relate to each other in the writer's creation of the story. You will learn a lot about the balance you need to strike in portraying all of your novel's characters.

Task Procedure:

> **Produce additional first-person biographies for all of the important minor Characters in your novel, especially the Antagonist(s).**

Remember to keep in mind the specific motives which are driving these characters to create the necessary tensions for the story. (See the previous checklist.)

Task Summary:

> **Select and develop the necessary cast for your novel's Central Conflict.**

Thomas Mann had little faith in his physical ability to sustain the emotional rigors of a truly creative life.

STEP FIVE

[The Story]

Task Procedure:

Create first drafts of Main Plot and Subplot Lines.

With your awareness of the premise, it's time to enlarge your story to what is called the *central conflict*. The central conflict is merely an expanded version of the elements incorporated in your premise. It forces you to begin to make more specific decisions about your story, but at the same time, it remains general enough to allow the necessary flexibility of invention which is so crucial at this stage in your story's development.

Task Procedure:

Write a Central Conflict for your novel.

You now need to form some specific ideas regarding your major and minor characters, and also some of the general actions of your story. At this point, you will choose the major conflict ingredients which are suggested by the premise. Some of these conflict ingredients include the plot shape and the cast of characters arrayed for and against the major character's goal. A central conflict is usually a page or two in length and puts in more interesting terms the elements which will eventually be dramatized. Fitzgerald's central conflict would have summarized Gatsby's character traits and basic position in society, as well as placed Daisy in her marriage with Tom Buchanan. Some of the minor characters like Jordan Baker and the Wilsons might have suggested themselves, but more likely Fitzgerald worked on the general setting and the type of people who would occupy it. It's also possible that he had not yet realized that he would need Nick Carraway as his narrator. It's important to remember to take your time and not push for too many details at this point. You want to make sure that the primary elements of your story are in place and beginning to suggest more supplementary ones.

Any such work you do on the construction of your story is referred to as a *blocking out*. You will do many such constructions before you're ready to actually start writing your novel. Each time you work with your blocking out, you will be refining your concept of the story's specifics, and this process will continue until you are ready to submit your novel for publication. Remember that the process of invention is not always orderly, so as you proceed through the next steps, be ready to foster a constantly questioning attitude. This healthy skepticism will encourage those discoveries which will aid you in building your plot and will result in your going back again and again to your original concepts and adapting them to your growing knowledge about your story. If you ever have the opportunity to look at the preliminary work of a successful author, you will probably be surprised. It's not uncommon for a story's final treatment (plot and character summaries) to be longer than the actual novel! But also remember to keep the procedure relatively simple at this stage and tell yourself to have patience. The beginning of a novel takes time, and it is time which is your best friend. If you try to move too fast, you will often skip necessary steps in the growth process, become discouraged by the difficulties you encounter and perhaps even quit. The secret is to set yourself accomplishable tasks, each of which leads naturally and easily to the next, so that before you know it, you have reached your goal.

Task Procedure:

Construct the Main Plot Line.

Take the expanded central conflict which you have just created and put that in front of you. Read it again and again, trying to get into the mind and heart of your major character in order to understand his/her most basic emotions. Write everything down that comes to you. Then go to the lists which you made that included the preliminary aspects of mystery, suspense and surprise. Again, read these over several times and take notes regarding any suggestions that they give you. Then with the plot shape in mind, pick a point where the forces aligned against your major character first appear. The major character may or may not be present, but regardless, for now this point is your opening scene. There's an old expression which applies here. Start your story as close to its end as you can. That may mean you have a story of 900 pages, but every page is necessary to the unraveling of the plot. For example, if you were to purchase a valuable painting and use it as a surprise attraction at a social gathering, you might cover the painting with butcher paper in order to hide it from your guests until the dramatic moment of unveiling. When you started to pull back the paper from the painting, only a small portion of one corner would be clear to the viewers, certainly not nearly enough of the painting for them to appreciate it or even understand what was portrayed. But when all the paper had been pulled away, your guests would also realize that the tiny portion which they had first glimpsed was certainly an integral part of the painting as a whole. That's where you should start your story: at the place and time of the *first important moment* which begins the process of the central conflict. You may choose the wrong moment, but don't worry about that. Later, you can go back and change it by starting your story at an earlier or later point. For now, it's important that you commit yourself to an actual choice. Subsequent discoveries cannot come from a vacuum. They will come when you start to make these early decisions regarding the primary ingredients of your novel.

Again, it's important to *not* be too detailed at this point. Just write down a few notes regarding the place and time of this suggested scene and in very general terms what the scene will show. In each of these specific moments, try to emphasize what will be accomplished that will cause tension for those involved and especially for your major character. You will see that you are using and reusing your mystery, suspense and surprise lists.

They will remind you of parts of your story which you will need to dramatize, and they will also suggest new ones.

Let's go back to our example story, *The Great Gatsby*. We can conjecture that the author Fitzgerald was by now realizing that his major character would need some help in achieving his goal of finding and perhaps regaining his lost love, Daisy Buchanan. The author probably decided that he wanted to keep his title character "off stage" for a while, to build up the mystery regarding his identity. Also at this point, Fitzgerald might have become convinced that he would definitely need another important character who might act not only as a helpmate in Gatsby's quest, but more importantly as a witness to the whole story. Fitzgerald's experience told him that his major character's desire would be quite clear to his readers, so that showing his internal state would be unnecessary. More importantly, revealing Gatsby's point of view might also be damaging to the suspense which he wanted to create later. In using a first-person narrator to "tell Gatsby's story," he Fitzgerald would gain several valuable things:

1. an objective witness who could be trusted to accurately report everything going on;
2. a mature somewhat distanced attitude which would help soften the otherwise heavy sentimentality of Gatsby's search;
3. another interesting character who would be involved in the story and who could therefore act as our medium of experiencing the events more fully than we could through Gatsby's rather obsessive point of view.

The author would thus have to open his novel at the point that the narrator (Nick Carraway) entered Gatsby's life, and invent a justification for this event to occur. What he came up with worked very well. Nick opens the novel by telling us that he had come East to learn the bond business. Nick eventually rents a small house next to Gatsby's property. The novel is thus launched at precisely the point at which the major character can attempt to succeed in obtaining the object of his desire via a series of surprising but not implausible circumstances connected to the narrator himself. Notice that the demands of forming the plot created an insight regarding the proper choice of point of view. In this way, two fictional devices worked together to show Fitzgerald what he needed to do.

Once you have chosen the opening scene of your novel, project the characters' motivations and resultant actions to the next logical event, remembering that you will probably go back later and change this original story line in many different ways. Simply let cause and effect carry you as far and as fast as you can in telling what is happening next. Go until you hit a snag (you may not!), and then go back and review what you have written so far. Also reread your original premise and central conflict, as well as the MSS lists. If nothing new is suggested, try to think of the ending for your novel, or what you want to have happen in terms of the outcome of the major character's central conflict. Then work backwards to the point where you hit the snag. If you encounter areas of the story that seem vague or confusing, just leave them alone for now. Most of the time, these kind of problems find their own solutions from later discoveries you will make. When you have most of the major character's actions in place, you have formed what is called the *main plot line*.

Task Procedure:

Construct the Subplot Lines.

No doubt, as you were working out what the major character was going to do, some suggestions came to you about actions for the minor characters, and especially the antagonist(s). You began to realize that in order for readers to fully appreciate the story, they had to be given glimpses of the minor characters' lives so as to understand the depth of the problem which the major character faced. In other words, all catalytic characters operate from recognizable motives that propel them to act to complicate the major character's life. You can therefore construct mini-stories within the major story to show us how these minor characters are acting from their own agendas, and not from some artificial motives of you the author. These antagonists will then have force when they act for or against the protagonist, and make your readers convinced of the reality of your story. When you create a series of actions or scenes for your minor characters, you are achieving what is called *subplot lines*.

In our make-believe example scenario with *The Great Gatsby*, Fitzgerald needed to build lives for his minor characters, and particularly for Daisy and Tom Buchanan. He needed Tom to be a cruel and materialistic person with a great deal of money and power, so that he would be a stark contrast to the considerate and romantic Gatsby. Fitzgerald, therefore, invented George and Myrtle Wilson. Tom Buchanan has an ongoing affair with Mrs. Wilson right under George's nose, and is exploiting them both for his own selfish ends. As the novel progresses, the author will be able to use these two desperate characters in other ways that will serve the plot. Another character, Jordan Baker, is created for several subplot reasons:

1. she acts as a vehicle of information for the narrator Nick Carraway;
2. she also represents just one more example of the callous and callow people who are surrounding the major character; and
3. she provides an important subplot function by helping the narrator bring Gatsby and Daisy together.

Take those minor characters (especially the antagonist[s]), for which you created biographies and write brief summaries of their primary actions in the story, highlighting their own personal motives/acts and how these motives/acts aid or block those of the major character. Later you will blend these subplots into the main plot line to make one unified and interesting story.

One important issue in the construction of your story is the balance between the withholding and the revelation of information. The process of telling any story is, in one simple way, the process of revealing information. But there are special pieces of information which will be revealed to your readers at those points in the story where they will best create tension There are also facts which, when revealed, will construct an increased tension. So in the invention of your story lines, you need to plan the points of revelation, when your characters and/or your readers will discover those tension elements needed to create or resolve the conflicts. Professional writers construct so-called revelation

STEP FIVE

charts which map out the exact points in the story line where key aspects of the characters' lives are to be revealed. In *The Great Gatsby*, for example, Fitzgerald had to pinpoint the place when Gatsby learns that Daisy is close at hand and willing to meet him. Given too soon or too late in the narrative, most revelations will lapse in the necessary tension and result in a reader's losing interest in the characters' actions.

Task Summary:

>**Create a general listing of the actions in your Main Plot Line and Subplot lines.**

Guy de Maupassant suffered from overwork and debauchery and was eventually overcome by insanity.

STEP SIX

[The Plot Structure]

Task Procedure:

> **Create a unified, interlocking series of Character actions.**

Publishers have told me that the most common defect which makes them reject novel manuscripts is a lack of *plot structure*. Structure, in general, means the way parts go together to make a whole. Engineers and architects work very hard to make the individual pieces of a bridge fit together so that the bridge can perform its function and not fall apart. In a novel, the same kind of unity is required. Fictional structure involves a perceptible arrangement of plot actions so that every event inevitably connects with past and future ones and also contributes to the formation of a complete story. In other words, each time a character acts, that action should be motivated by plausible (seen or unseen) causes which precede it. These causes must be consistent with the criteria established by you the author. The character actions in *The Great Gatsby* meet one kind of criteria, whereas the character actions in *Alice In Wonderland* meet another.

However, plot actions need to be more than just causally connected. They also need to be dramatic. If you are working from a concept of one or more plot shapes, then you have already achieved an "automatic" drama in your story. You now need to start thinking in terms of specific character actions which will continue the initial interest created by these plot shapes. Dramatic actions come from characters with conflicting desires. You need to take the specific subplot lines which you have already completed and begin to merge them with the main plot line. In *The Great Gatsby*, Fitzgerald created a separate plot line for Tom Buchanan, Gatsby's rival for Daisy. Tom's actions with Myrtle Wilson inevitably involve Gatsby with George Wilson, and this connection eventually leads to Gatsby's death. Below, I will show you how to achieve this blending of all the plot lines, but first you need to know a few more things about plot structure.

In general, there are two kinds of plot structure: *episodic* and *cumulative.* If each scene in a novel can stand relatively alone as a kind of mini-story with its own climax, an episodic structure is being used. On the other hand, if each scene requires an understanding of what precedes it to be fully understood, then a cumulative structure is being used. In the cumulative structure, each scene is more an outgrowth of its predecessor than a coherent whole on its own. Seldom do you find an extreme example of either episodic or cumulative structure. For now, try to make sure that all of your characters act from their own recognizable motives. The material itself will probably make it clear to you which kind of structure you are working toward. As you were completing your preliminary plot lines (main and subplot), you were learning to see the natural relationships of the actions you chose for your characters.

In order to achieve an effective plot structure, you will also need to understand how narrative actions are rendered. Here two general techniques that can help you: *scene* and *summary.*

Scene is the close-up view, and it is created by an author's presentation of immediate, specific details regarding the characters' actions, speech, and physical appearance, as well as setting. You know that stage plays and movies are made up of scenes. These dramas are presented directly to a viewing audience. Obviously, because of the intervention of the written word, fiction writers must relate what is happening on their "stage" indirectly. It is much like having the audience's view of the events being blocked by a sound proof curtain. You the author (as "witness" of the events) must tell your audience what is happening on your "stage." Hopefully, you will relate these events in as much physical detail as you can, so that the audience can become involved in them, and thus come to care about their culmination or climax. Not all actions in a novel warrant specific dramatization, and there are also times when a writer wants to "hurry up" the story's progress and pass the narrative time quickly. At such times, the author uses summary.

Summary implies a more distanced view, but it is not a generalized version of the events being rendered. Longer periods of time and a multiplicity of events are compressed into brief passages by three basic techniques called *methods of compression:* subsequent action, typical action, and symbolic action.

Subsequent Action

This technique involves the presentation of actions that imply that prior actions had to be performed first. If a character is listening to the radio to hear some important news pertinent to the plot, you would not have to report his/her turning on the radio first. In rendering minor actions in your novel, make sure that you're not reporting details for the sake of doing so, or using them to "convince" your reader of the reality of your story. Instead, try to move quickly to those actions which are most dramatically important and let those suggest the preceding ones.

Typical Action

This technique involves the presentation of a few details to stand for many, or a typical detail to imply something more general which it is related to. You can dramatize your character's life during a period of time by suggesting a few meaningful actions, especially those which were practiced routinely. As someone once said, to describe a tree, you don't need to describe every leaf.

Symbolic Action

This technique involves the presentation of a single, striking action which has previously been developed to give off a powerful meaning. You can then repeat the action where it will be noticed and remind the reader of the larger meaning that is being suggested.

What all three of these methods have in common is their emphasis on the selection of something stated to imply something not stated. By using them, you can both move the story quickly without losing the reader's sense of participation and also not bog down the story by giving needless details. A judicious use of scene and summary in a proper balance will help you shorten your story when immediate drama is not demanded and expand it where drama is present.

In general, there is a logical formula for the handling of scene and summary. A novel will probably open in scene, but then move quickly to brief portions of summary when more general or background information is needed. The novel will then continue to present a series of scene and summary passages, moving toward an ever more specific rendering. The logic for this pattern is evident. As readers become more acquainted with your characters and their conflicts, they will want to share more specifically in their lives. The climax or climactic scene is, of course, the place where you will be obligated to present the events in a very detailed manner. Naturally not all novels follow this general formula, but most do.

One element remains to help you achieve the right balance between a specific and a general rendering of events, and it is called *half-scene*. The term half-scene does not mean fifty percent of a scene. It involves using a few details to briefly interrupt a summary passage. You will give your readers the impression that they are intimately experiencing your characters' lives, while you will also be quickly moving your story along.

Here is a typical example that employs the h technique:

John and Mary were so busy at their respective jobs that they forgot to see that their marriage was falling apart. They often ate alone from warmed up plastic food in plastic cartons, staring at flickering TV screens. At night one or the other was too tired to make love, and most mornings went by in a caffeine-filled daze of anticipations of the day. It was a particular rainy Sunday in March that they looked at each other, and John said it for the both of them. "I think we need a vacation." The wrinkles around her eyes seemed to relax. "A penetrating observation, counselor." He took her hand and held it for several seconds, picked up the phone and told his secretary he wouldn't be coming in to the office that day. Three hours later they were packed and on their way to the airport.

Notice that in the above example, the author begins with a summary of the general situation between the two characters, and this summary leads to a brief dialogue and action exchange which in turn leads to another summary passage. In your reading of fiction, try to spot the half-scenes, and analyze how the writer moves in and out of summary to make the reader feel closer to the drama.

It should be noted that scene and summary affect the pace of a novel by determining how long it takes the reader to read a particular passage. Whereas scene slows your novel's pace, summary speeds it up. You can cover more time and space more quickly while using summary, but at the same time, your scenes will be the most interesting parts of your novel and should therefore dominate as the major structural device. In order to write effective scenes, you need to keep the following four criteria in mind:

1. Scenes should occur at key conflicting moments in the plot where details are necessary to create drama.

2. Scenes should be representative of life and live up to the normal demands of time and space unless you are writing in a nonrealistic genre.

3. Scenes should complete a definite dramatic point in the story's development (when a story is moving forward by presenting new information to the reader, it is said to be *advancing*).

4. Scenes should have new ingredients in them and not repeat situations that have already been dramatized.

Task Procedure:

Complete a second blocking out by listing specific scenes in both the Main Plot Lines and the Subplot Lines.

You will want to make this second blocking out a listing of those scenes which may eventually be used in your story. Reread your notes which you made in response to previous chapters (especially those regarding your premise and central conflict) and then go back to the plot lines which you wrote for your first blocking out.

Using these brief summaries as guides, start fresh by titling your screen or paper with the words: main plot line (specific scenes). If you haven't done this before, make a choice of where you think the novel should begin and put that choice down as the first item on your list.

Then by continuing to refer to your prior notes, cite subsequent scenes which your major character will need in order to achieve what he/she wants. You will, of course, integrate the actions of your other, minor characters as aids or blocks to the major character, and continue to list your major character's reactions to them. While inventing these scenes, try to stick to believable motives and acts, but at the same time, remember to look for original or surprising actions which will add to your concept of the characters.

No procedure like this one can or should be formularized, but you will probably see how you will work most comfortably when you are working within the boundaries which you yourself have laid down. There will be many discoveries and counter discoveries which will come from your earlier ones. Also, do not be dismayed if you end up later completely changing what you are inventing now. Remember to console yourself with this truth: you will not have these later, more useful discoveries *unless you first make the earlier ones*! Especially in the creative process, you need to patiently involve yourself in a series of trial-and-error commitments, each one made and discarded, leading you naturally to an eventual and successful conclusion.

Once you have gone as far as you can with the scenes in the main plot line (and there may be gaps along the way), go to those subplot lines which you have developed through the use of your minor antagonists. Create similar lists for all of these. Initially you will draw upon those scenes you have already developed in the main plot line, but you will also discover additional ones. Of course, remember that the actions of your minor characters must always serve the development of the central conflict and not be in the story for their own sake.

Again, using our sample novel, *The Great Gatsby*, let us pretend that Fitzgerald is following my system and guess that his early blocking out might have looked something like the following:

Main Plot Line (specific scenes)

"After serving in WWI and graduating from college (probably Yale), have Nick C. come to New York to work in some line (make this in banking or something like that), N. rents a house which coincidentally adjoins Gatsby's.

"Here show him taking up again with his cousin who just happens to be Daisy Buchanan, the woman Gatsby is desperately looking for, have him meet Daisy and her husband Tom at their place, or maybe at a party, also at this party or whatever, Nick meets a possible love of his own, Jordan Baker, somehow he learns what an SOB Tom is (this is important for later in motivating Daisy and Gatsby to try to get together), for instance, maybe Tom is having an affair with some lower-class woman and Jordan tells N. about this.

"Next scene could be at this woman's place, she's also married to some car mechanic or whatever, and Tom egotistically invites our narrator along with Baker and his own wife!! No. . . scratch the wife, not necessary or believable for Daisy to be along, have a crude, raucous party showing how the rich do it and show Tom's incredible disregard for goodness and/or his marriage, end scene by Tom's breaking something, maybe his girl friend's nose.

"Not sure about what comes next, but now need to switch more attention onto Gatsby, what he's been doing to find Daisy, a good vehicle might be showing an ongoing lavish party which G. keeps going, hoping Daisy will someday drop in by accident (remember, he doesn't know where Daisy is although the reader does, because of Nick)."

Well, my apologies to the spirit of F. Scott Fitzgerald, but you the reader of this book can see how it works. At this point, the writer is feeling his/her way along, trying to use the elements of the early planning stage, while still being alert to new suggestions. Fitzgerald could also have written a similar scene outline for Tom Buchanan, including the scene above, filling out all of Tom's key actions in the book, especially the fatal, culminating one.

Within this system, the best ingredients of the creative process are invited to work together, while still building in you the confidence that you are working on something which is based on a solid foundation. When you have finished each of the separate plot lines, you need to get away from the mind-set which this early invention period requires and let some time pass. Notice that you have not yet decided very much about the specific details of the scenes you have listed. In fact, in some cases you have deliberately avoided being too specific. Leaving these more particular decisions to be made later, you have resisted the anxiety to tell your complete story now, and therefore left your perceptive energies free to focus where they should—on the overall choice and sequencing of the scenes necessary to dramatize your story. You will be acting much like the artist who takes a piece of charcoal and sketches out the broader outlines of what he/she thinks might be in the finished painting. In not being too specific, you have also left much in the way of necessary invention to be accomplished later and have thus guaranteed yourself further enjoyment in the ongoing process of creating your novel. Writing a novel is like a long-distance run. It requires emotional and psychological endurance on your part. If the writing process can also be fun, you will take the time and energy to do it well.

Having let some time pass, now go back to all of your individual plot lines and reread them, keeping your original plot premise and central conflict in mind. Now revise these lists to eliminate redundant or needless scenes, moving events around which are not timed effectively, adding ones to enhance the overall dramatic impact, and modifying those which are not yet what you want them to be. If you had not completed them before, try to do so now, remembering that an effective climax should evolve naturally from the scenes that precede it and not be an arbitrary decision on your part. If any gaps or uncertain areas remain in your plot lines, don't worry about them. They will most likely clarify themselves later.

Task Summary:

       Create a scene-by-scene blocking out for all Plot Lines.

Franz Kafka gained a law degree but never used it, suffered all of his life because of powerful feelings of inferiority and the disease of tuberculosis.

STEP SEVEN

[The Plot Elements]

Task Procedure:

Deepen your concept of Plot usages.

Before doing a final version of the plot structure, you need to think about four additional concepts which will apply to your novel. These elements will help you construct a more appealing story, as well as suggest ways you can revise the discoveries you have already made. These concepts are: *aesthetic distance, time usages, tone,* and *pace.* Let's look at them one at a time.

Aesthetic Distance

In my discussion of scene and summary, I pointed out that scene makes readers feel closer to your characters and summary farther away. The element which really accounts for these feelings is called aesthetic distance. Aesthetic distance deals with the subjective ability of a human being to associate with what he/she is experiencing. Literally translated it means "art distance," and it mainly applies to situations when a person is an observer of an artistic endeavor. For instance, when you are sitting in a theater watching a murder on the stage, you do not run up on the stage to stop the murder. To the extent that you realize that this action is part of the play, you have allowed aesthetic distance to affect your behavior. Aesthetic distance also applies to experiences which are outside artistic arenas. As a passenger on the doomed Titanic, you might have pointed out your artistic appreciation of that "beautiful, shiny blue thing on the horizon," until someone else mentioned to you that it was an iceberg that could sink the ship. Your artistic pleasure would quickly be replaced by a sense of realistic concern.

The concept of aesthetic distance affects the actual writing process more than it does the planning process, but it is an important issue in any preliminary planning because it helps you discover those most intimate moments which you will need to dramatize. Let's see more specifically how aesthetic distance works in fiction writing.

When you are watching a play or movie, there is less aesthetic distance between you and what's happening on the stage or screen, especially in more realistic dramas. But because of the barrier of the written word, your readers will find various degrees of difficulty identifying with your characters as you describe them. You will eventually have to decide whether you want your readers to "become" your characters, observe them from a more objective perspective, or participate in some kind of combination of both stances.

Many other factors will affect this reader identification, but the most powerful factor is point of view. As you know, there are various points of view. In general, first-person achieves the least amount of aesthetic distance (stronger reader identification with your characters), and third-person omniscient the most amount of aesthetic distance (weaker reader identification). Aesthetic distance is never constant because various moments in your story will have different dramatic importance. For example, in *The Great Gatsby*, there is much greater distance in the scene when Gatsby is giving his lavish party than in the scene when Gatsby is reuniting with his lost love, Daisy Buchanan.

Even after you have chosen a particular point of view for your novel, you need to consider another element which will affect aesthetic distance. *Character referencing* will also help determine how close your readers will feel to your characters. The chart below represents what I call the "Distance Factor." (A hint: read it from the bottom up)

Revision Stance —	Writer	+	Reader
			Man
			Worker
[referencing words]			Husband
			John
			He
			I
First Draft Stance—	Writer	=	Character(s)

During the first draft, the writer and the characters are like one entity. In essence, you the writer *are* your characters. You are like an actor playing all the roles in a stage play; there should be relatively little objectivity on your part, so that you can *become* the people you are representing. In contrast, during the revisionary stance, you will leave behind this close subjective identification with your characters and become the objective, revising artist, gauging your accomplishment and shaping it to fit your artistic concerns. Of course, the third and very important member in this situation is the reader. What will the reader do in this identification process? The answer is simple in theory, if not in practice. In terms of aesthetic distance, the reader's reaction to your characters will depend upon how you refer to them.

Your readers are, as it were, on an elevator, being moved up and down according to your use of referencing nouns and pronouns. As the chart implies, the first-person pronoun is the most intimate referencing possible, making your readers closely identify with your characters. As you go up the chart to the subsequent references (only typical samples), you make the reader feel farther away from your characters. Test this for yourself. Start at the top of the list and read the following lines, allowing time to pass between each one, and see how, as a reader, you will feel the distance increasing between you and the performing character.

>I walked into the room and saw her.
>He walked into the room and saw her.
>John walked into the room and saw her.
>The husband walked into the room and saw her.
>The worker walked into the room and saw her.
>The man walked into the room and saw her.
>The individual walked into the room and saw her.
>Someone walked into the room and saw her.

Each line provides a different impression and gains a different response from the reader, but the crucial choice lies between the second and third lines. Many writers will inadvertently keep referring to their characters by their names, instead of using the appropriate pronouns, and thus unknowingly push their readers away from a closer identification. In contrast, a heavy use of pronouns will keep the reader as close to the scene or summary as possible and enlarge the dramatic impact of the actions being presented. Thus, the referencing process is just one more means to control your readers' responses to your story.

Time Usages

Now that you are working your way gradually to a finished plot structure, you need to think about the relationship of time as it relates to the actions your characters will be performing. As I said above, time in the broadest sense is really an element of setting because all elements of place are affected by the time in history in which they occur. Time also affects plot because the rendering of action uses up time, and so you need to consider time when structuring your events.

First, let us remember that there are two kinds of time: natural (objective) time, and experiential (subjective time). In the natural world, no matter what you name it or how you measure it, an "hour" is still an hour. But time being experienced by a human being is a very different matter. Depending on what you're doing during any particular time period, the time will seem to move at different rates of speed. In constructing your plot structure, you need to account for both kinds of time, and not invent sequences of action that could not take place because of time discrepancies. I once read a story which presented a scene in which two characters took a cab from Kennedy Airport to downtown Manhattan, and according to the objective rendering of the scene, the cab ride took only ten minutes, an impossibility in any circumstances. Of course, the writer could have shown the two characters so wrapped up in their own conversation (or whatever!!), that to them the ride seemed just "minutes long."

Another consideration of time is the so-called *time zone*. How long your novel lasts in the life of your major character is the time zone for your novel. It may be as short as a few hours or days, or as long as two or three generations. "Start your story as close to the end as possible" is an old saying that relates here. The prescription suggests that the shortest amount of time possible should be used in constructing your time zone. This time restriction will give your story force because nothing will be narrated that isn't actually essential to the central conflict. Thus, the reader's concentration will be focused on the fewest possible things. If you want to include portions of a character's childhood, you don't have to start the novel when the character is a child. You can suggest the childhood indirectly in aspects of his/her adult life, or you can *flashback* to that one period, dramatize it, and then come forward again to the more recent time. Time manipulation can be a complex issue, but you will learn to recognize how to achieve effective time usage as you are writing your book.

In structuring your plot, you should also consider how you are going to order or pattern the time in the actual rendering because this factor will affect the final blocking out. Most conventional or traditional novels are told in a *chronological* time pattern. That is, one event follows another in a logical sequence, and once a certain time is passed, the readers' attention is done with it. A more experimental time usage is the *overlapping* time pattern. A multiple character point of view usually accompanies this pattern, whereby the author relates several different versions of the same time period from differing character perspectives. There are other, more flamboyant time usages, but you need not concern yourself with them now. In your reading, especially of more modern fiction, you can study and analyze the way the authors employ time, and through this study, you can learn to apply more complex techniques.

A final time consideration is more related to the actual writing of your novel, but to be complete, I will discuss it here. You will need to find ways to pass the time in the narrative, so that your readers can relate to your characters' actions. The usual ways of passing time are:

Implications of Scene and Summary
Pure Statement
Space Breaks

Obviously, as I stated earlier, the rendering of scene and summary takes up a certain amount of time, no matter what is going on. We also know that scene takes up less time in the characters' lives because it is more detailed, and conversely, summary hurries the story along. Occasionally, however, the writer may want to move the story even more quickly and will then be able to use a variety of statements which tell the reader directly about the amount of time that has passed. Some typical examples might be:

Soon after that, he. . .
At ten that night, he . . .
The next day he . . .
It was the following summer that he . . .
Five years passed until he saw him again on . . .

Readers are accustomed to seeing such informational insertions without actually paying too much attention to them. Judiciously used, they keep the story going and help you to avoid rendering events which do not contribute to the central conflict.

Space breaks are also a handy way to imply passages of time, either within chapters or at the end of chapters. Most readers understand that the empty space represents a certain passage of time. Finally, remember that you will learn how much time is required in the story, and within that time zone, when and where to move the story and how fast. Your job is to be alert to the factors of time as they affect and are affected by the elements of your novel.

Tone

In all writing contexts, *tone* means the attitude(s) the writer has toward his/her own purpose, subject matter, and audience. Tone might vary from an air of silly amusement to one of morose seriousness. There are obviously many possible attitudes and mixtures of attitudes. In a long story like a novel, you will usually want to achieve a variety of tonal effects, so that your readers don't become bored. In *The Great Gatsby*, admittedly a very serious and eventually tragic story, there are still elements of lighthearted humor and even satire. Fitzgerald has written a story of individual foolishness and naiveté, but he has also created a scathing criticism of his times, and especially of the rich people whose careless disregard for each other bothered him deeply.

Tone is achieved by what you choose to write about and how you choose to write it. Any fictional subject may be treated with different tonal effects. Looked at from one perspective, even the saddest event can be made the topic of humor, or vice versa. So, you will have to decide in advance what tonal approach to take in regards to your premise and central conflict. Look for opportunities during the final blocking out (Step Nine) to find varieties of tone, perhaps releasing the reader from a series of very tense and serious episodes by going to a background event. Often, a minor character with some kind of quirky personality trait can offer moments of humorous release from otherwise somber actions. There are no magic formulas which I can cite to insure the proper use of tone. My best advice is to allow time to pass between original and subsequent drafts and remind yourself during the revision process to pay special attention to this element. Other readers can also help you pick up tonal discrepancies or inconsistencies.

Pace

Officially, *pace* is defined as the amount of words (i.e., space) a writer uses in proportion to the amount of details which are given to the reader. As I mentioned before, scene slows the pace of a story, whereas summary speeds it up. "Variety is the spice of life," is a familiar quote from William Shakespeare, and it is certainly true in regards to this fictional element. Readers will be worn out by events being rendered at the same pace throughout a book. As in life, we want to experience some moments, perhaps emotionally powerful ones, with a slow, painstaking appreciation of every single innuendo present. On the other hand, not every moment warrants such a rigorous presentation. There will be many time periods in your story which should be passed quickly, so you can use the methods of compression mentioned before to increase the pace. Most readers will also appreciate a fast pace at the beginning of the novel while they are getting acquainted with your characters and their conflicts, and also, ironically, at the end of the novel when they are anxious to get to the exciting resolution of these conflicts. Naturally, there are many possible varieties of pace which will be appropriate to any given novel. You should be sensitive to this element in your original plotting and build into the plot structure places where the pace slows or speeds up in contrast to what has preceded. This variation in pace will serve you greatly while you manipulate various characters through their necessary actions and also help you gain differences in tone which I mentioned above.

One final note in regards to pace. While constructing your sequence of plot actions, try to avoid "going too quickly to the target." This is a metaphoric way of saying that if you present the need for an upcoming action, so that your reader is anxious to see it happen, do not immediately dramatize that action. Make the reader wait somewhat by going to another scene which will contribute to future conflicts, perhaps one from a subplot line. After having had a brief respite from the tensions involved, the reader will be all the more refreshed and thus excited about sharing the big moment. This technique also gives the reader a subtle message: you are in charge here and you do not intend to make your story predictable in any way!

Task Summary:

    Apply the principles of Aesthetic Distance, Time Usage, Tone and Pace to your story.

Edgar Allan Poe was dismissed from West Point because of his reputation for heavy drinking and gambling.

STEP EIGHT

[The Complete Blocking Out]

Task Procedure:

    Write a detailed summary version of your entire story, with all the Characters' actions sequenced and motivated as they will be dramatized in your novel.

    After completing the above, choose your Point of View Character(s).

    You need to make one more technical choice before finalizing your complete story. In Step Two, I defined point of view and briefly discussed some of its attributes. In order to choose the one point of view which you will use in your novel, you need to consider the general advantages and disadvantages of each of the possible choices. Point of view, remember, is the character's voice and not the author's voice. When a character is referred to in a narrative line, a certain pronoun is eventually used, and that pronoun indicates the point of view type. As we know, two points of view dominate in traditional fiction, first-person and third-person. The following are the more or less conventional choices available:

First-Person:
    There are three first-person points of view, all using the pronoun "I":

1. Major Character;
2. Minor Character; and
3. Observer.

The first two are self-explanatory. When an "I" voice renders the actions, but in no way participates in the story, we have the third choice. All three points of view have the same basic advantages and disadvantages.

Advantages
1. Intimacy: a first-person witness relates the story more directly to the reader, making it easier for the reader to identify with that character.
2. Authenticity: a first-person witness tends to be more credible.
3. Flexibility: a first-person witness can more easily relate events that go back and forth in time and switch from place to place.
4. Immediacy: a first-person witness seems to be more involved in the present drama. The old "You Are There" radio/TV programs used such a narrator.

Disadvantages
1. Narrow Viewpoint: the first-person witness presents only one version of the story's events.
2. Less Objectivity: a first-person character tends to report events more subjectively and with fewer external details.
3. Materialization: a first-person character will not come across as clearly (materialize) because he/she is viewing others and no one is viewing him/her.

Third-Person
This point of view contributes the widest possible perspective to your story. Third-person is generally easier to use because it is closer to the author's voice, and works best in novels with many characters whose actions are important to the plot. There are three choices of third-person point of view:

1. Single Character (Limited or Central): this point of view is probably most common in fiction writing because it provides

the most advantages with the fewest number of disadvantages. It presents the story from only one character's awareness, and this singular perspective tends to encourage a presentation of those aspects of the story which are most important. In general, all the advantages and disadvantages of first-person are also present in this point of view, except that there is less aesthetic distance between the first-person character and your readers than in the third-person single character. On the other hand, a major advantage of third-person single character is that you can move from the third-person voice to your author's voice, whereas you cannot normally go to an author's stance, once the first-person (I-voice) has been established. Once Nick Carraway has been established as the first-person narrator in *The Great Gatsby,* Fitzgerald maintains that stance throughout the novel. There have been certain experimental usages which have mixed various points of view, but I don't recommend that you try any of these applications until you have gained considerable writing experience.

2. Multiple Character (Omniscient): this choice contributes the widest possible perspective to your story. When the awareness of two or more characters is reported, this point of view takes effect. When compared to first-person point of view, all the advantages and disadvantages become reversed. Multiple character point of view is obviously the most flexible because you will never be at a loss for a potential point of view character. Plot manipulation is also easier because you can switch to any scene you want to without having to worry if your one point of view character would plausibly inhabit that scene. On the other hand, because of the many-sided versions which readers will receive, they will not feel as close to any one of your characters, thus increasing the aesthetic distance between them and your story. You can imagine how differently you would relate to *The Great Gatsby* if it were told from Nick's, Daisy's, Tom's and Gatsby's points of view. You would have a fuller story in one sense, but not the same type of story Fitzgerald told.

3. Effaced Narrator (Camera Eye): This somewhat unique point of view presents an entirely objective or external view of the characters' actions Like a sound camera, the unknown, god-

like narrator's voice gives only the surfaces of outward reality and never tells directly what the characters are thinking or feeling. This choice naturally presents a high degree of realism while at the same time de-emphasizes a character's internal conflicts. Readers may quickly identify with the authenticity of your story, but may also have a problem intimately identifying with your characters' more complex desires.

Which choice you make should be determined by the specific factors of your story. If you think about it carefully, you will be able to choose that point of view which best allows the drama to come across to your readers. My advice is to start with the simplest, most obvious choices until they show you that they are somehow limiting your ability to tell your story. I would not recommend that you arbitrarily pick a more complex choice just because it seems attractive. Like all your technical choices in writing your novel, let the characters tell you which choice seems the best. You can always change it later.

The point of view of *The Great Gatsby* has been the source of much critical debate over the years because it is so unique. Nick Carraway is the first-person narrator, but he does not seem like a traditional major character. Neither can you call him the typical minor character since he participates in important events that help shape the plot's outcome. Moreover, Jay Gatsby himself, whose point of view we never share, is definitely not the typical major character. He is the title character, and admittedly, it is his obsession that drives the story, but he never understands why he himself is the cause of the conflict, so he never changes. On the other hand, Nick is vastly changed by the events and of course outlives Gatsby at the end. You might accurately conclude that taken together, Carraway and Gatsby form a kind of major character "entity," and that Fitzgerald ultimately made an excellent point of view choice. Nick is a tolerant, relatively objective witness who can be trusted to tell us what we need to know. Moreover, seeing inside Gatsby's mind would have served no purpose because it is Gatsby's outward behavior that speaks eloquently for him. Beyond that, listening to Gatsby's thoughts would only defuse the drama because we would have to know that he never did understand his fatal mistake, and this insight might make us impatient with Gatsby and tire of the events which bring him to his climactic end.

Now go through your merged plot lines (both main and subplot), looking at every scene in order to determine who the point of view character has to be. When you are through (and perhaps long before that!), you will know which of the point of view choices seems to be the right one. You may have to modify certain scenes in terms of who, what, when and where, in order to adapt your point of view choice to your earlier plot choices. Feel confident that any apparent confusion will generally clarify itself as you continue to work on your novel. Do not over react to any temporary problem which cannot be immediately solved. That is the best part of this system. Built into it is a growing confidence on your part that you have already made the necessary discoveries to get this far; there's every reason to believe that you will continue to do so.

Task Procedure:

Complete the final blocking out.

This blocking out sometimes takes many forms. No matter what you call it, or how you choose to complete it, this blocking out will incorporate all the planning and discoveries which you have made up to this point. It will by no means be a finished product (you will continue to plan and discover as you write your book), but it *is* the last truly preliminary map you will write for the journey that lies ahead of you.

Although there are many ways to complete this step, I recommend that you write a complete prose-like rendering of your story in all of its specifics, using your scene-by-scene listings as guides. Remember: you are *not yet* actually applying fiction writing techniques, but are relating the characters' motives and acts in a general, "telling" stance. Specifics of character action, dialogue, physical appearance and setting may intrude, and if they do, I recommend that you write them down. But feel no obligation whatsoever to be specific in the way you will need to be when you actually dramatize these events. Be aware, that even though you may have planned your story very meticulously over a long time, new discoveries, fine-tuning adjustments, will also continue to come, and it is very important to incorporate them in this overall narrative structure. It is possible that you will do several versions of this final story summary until you feel every piece is exactly in place. In fact, you should have the patience to *not* be satisfied if any part of your story does not ring true to you. You need to listen to your "voice" now more than ever. Realization of a solid plot structure will give you the necessary confidence to complete and revise your novel.

If you have the money, you might want to show this blocking out to a professional writing consultant or so-called "book doctor." A good professional appraisal could save you many hours of wasted effort and improve your novel greatly.

This is the moment you have been waiting for. Rest assured that you have done everything humanly possible to get ready for it. And don't forget to enjoy yourself! The actual writing process may seem frightening, but you *can* accomplish it! Persevere with patience and faith, and don't forget to keep your mind open for those magical suggestions which are sure to come. As I have suggested before, the writing of a novel is a partnership. You don't have to feel all alone. Get the various kinds of help you need and never give up!

What follows is a brief sample of how F. Scott Fitzgerald might have responded to this Step if he had been a reader of this book. His final blocking out might have started something like this:

"I will open with a kind of statement by Nick that reveals his essential character. This will be necessary to establish a base for all the rest of his observations and convince the reader that he can be trusted. He will be returning from the Middle West to East Egg and the corruption and purposelessness of long time wealth. He will rent a modest bungalow adjoining the huge mansions of the rich, neighboring Gatsby's estate. Next have an opening party, basically casual, but big enough to attract the reader and characterize those attending. Tom, Daisy and Jordan Baker are present, and Nick will narrate the immediate details, as well as learn about Daisy and Tom, and Tom's mistress. He will also meet Jordan Baker and perhaps be initially attracted. This party will establish the necessary facts of Daisy's presence and availability even before the reader knows it's important to Gatsby. After the party, Nick returns to his modest home and catches a glimpse of Gatsby alone on the dock, reaching his arms out toward the single green light that is the visible symbol for his obsession. At this point, Nick only views Gatsby; he does not encounter him or know who he really is. This will probably be the end of Chapter One. Chapter Two will begin with . . . ."

Task Summary:

> **Write a complete blocking out for your entire novel, and then choose a preliminary Point of View.**

**D. H. Lawrence was victimized
by a suffocating relationship with his mother
and could not write for two years after she died.**

STEP NINE

[The Opening Chapter]

Task Procedure:

Write an opening chapter for your novel.

Times have changed since the days of F. Scott Fitzgerald and *The Great Gatsby*. In Fitzgerald's time and in previous generations, novels could begin leisurely, slowly presenting the setting, the major character's background, and perhaps several sketches of minor characters, before beginning to reveal the key points of the central conflict. As I have implied earlier from my discussion of premise and other plot factors, present-day writers simply cannot afford the luxury of such slow-paced beginnings. For several decades, our readers have been conditioned by movies and television, as well as the overall fast pace of life in the twentieth century. The results are obvious.

Readers today want a fast-moving, action-oriented story with a strong visual appeal, so agents and publishers are naturally responding to these demands by accepting those scripts that foster a well structured plot and several supporting subplots, as well as an accessible style. Of course, you may want to write a story which does not fulfill this commercial criteria; there is a small but persistent market for books which are not written according to any formula. You have to decide what kind of story you want to tell and be true to that concept no matter what. On the other hand, before you discard the suggestions I am about to make, you might try to see if they can be adopted within your approach.

Remember that even William Shakespeare had to be cognizant of his less than literate audience. It is doubtful that this, perhaps the greatest writer of all time, would have ever found an acceptance for his great wisdom unless he had dramatized it through very "commercial" plots and interesting characters. In a final sense, your novel is a collaboration. You and your readers are together creating the story. Without you, there would be no story to read; without them, there will be no story to exist.

I recommend the following steps for your first chapter:

1. Go back to your final blocking out and make sure that your opening scene is as close to the end of your novel as possible. Also make sure that it dramatizes the moment when the central conflict first begins. *Do not start your story with the following items!*

- a) Summary information about your characters' past or present lives.
- b) Scenes which merely establish your characters' personalities.
- c) Descriptions of setting for their own sake.
- d) Narrations which attempt to "prove" that you know your subject matter.

Remember that your job is to make the reader's job worth the effort by instantly providing elements of mystery which will in turn offer opportunities for suspense and surprise. The writing of fiction is the writing of performance. In fact, it could be helpful at this stage of your writing to picture how your opening scene would look if it were in a movie or television drama. Visualize those specific factors which the camera would focus on in order to immediately create tension for the viewing audience. Some of these factors may be subtle and more deeply appreciated later, but there needs to be enough conflict to draw the reader in and make him/her keep turning the pages. *Do start your story with the following items:*

A first line which grabs the reader and forces him/her to read the next line, and the next, and the next. This first line is the most important line in your novel. It should refer to something external and real and not be a line of pure thought or feeling which might be vague or ambiguous. It should also "arrest the moment" or appear to break into already ongoing action. You have seen stage plays in which the curtain opens on human life which seems to be "interrupted" by your presence in the theater. This sense of subtle intrusion into the life of the characters is crucial in initiating a series of quiet revolutions within the psyche of your reader. After all, your reader has just paid $39.95 of his/her hard-earned money for your book! He/she has taken a seat on a crowded and noisy metro train and opened your book to page one. There are also a myriad of other distractions: worries about unpaid bills or that night's blind date; anticipations of next week's big meeting or the next month's visit of a mother-in-law; memories of last summer's vacation or the death of a loved one. You get the idea. Human life is filled with good reasons *not* to become involved in your story. Thankfully, it is also filled with good reasons to do so, or writers, agents and publishers would be out of business. We read books to experience mystery, suspense and surprise. There is also the realization that when we read, we are able to enlarge our lives, enjoy experiences and learn about ourselves in ways normally prohibited by life's realities. So . . . that first line must first literally jerk us out of the realistic mind set which all of us occupy and take us quickly to a new and exciting world which you have created. This line and those that follow it also make a promise: keep reading and you won't be sorry. You the writer are saying, "Don't worry. I am not going to bore you with a lot of fancy speeches, dull philosophies or hackneyed situations. My characters will be exciting and interesting and real. My settings will be exotic even if they are like your very own neighborhoods. And I will entertain you and enlighten you and make you glad that you paid your money and made the effort to join me in this, the world I created for you." Whew! That's a lot to ask of just a few lines. How can you accomplish all that?

    To make your opening line compelling, incorporate in it a note of tension or conflict which will pique your reader's curiosity—perhaps an odd or unexpected fact:

> "As the plane taxied toward the terminal, he looked out the

window and received a shock. This wasn't Tucson. He was coming home, but that terminal wasn't familiar at all!"

Or perhaps something appealing to several senses at once:
"The smoke from the fire made him cough as he crawled through the searing grass, but just ahead of him was the glistening black surface of the stream, and somewhere, crazily lost in his memory, the deep forlorn moan of a foghorn."

Or perhaps a striking action or dialogue:
"He took the pot of boiling soup and went to the sink and poured it down the drain while she watched, a smile slowly forming across her startled face."

Or another version:
"'You said you were going to kill me. So do it!'"

Or perhaps a thought which reveals a powerful emotion that cannot be denied:
"He looked at her from across the room and knew that by nightfall she would beg him to sleep with her."

In all these lines, I have used the character's own concern to try to attract the reader's concern. There are, of course, countless such lines available, but you also need to make sure that they are not artificial or falsely promising of what is to follow. My lines above do not come from any deep sense of character and plot, but yours must. Invent that moment when your major character is first confronted with an awareness which will become inevitable. Your job in blocking out your novel is to create a world in which your major character cannot avoid his/her fate. In the first line, you begin to unfold the actions which will create that confrontation.

2. Continue to make your opening scene compelling by allowing the characters to react freely to the tension elements which you have placed there. Put down everything that comes to mind. Let your imagination have full reign and push your characters to act and speak in ways which will reveal their inner emotions. Don't make speeches directly (author's voice) or indirectly (character voice) *about* the conflict in the scene. Dramatize it through a judicious use of concrete and specific details. Have faith that these details will imply what you want

them to. Remember that you are in the final analysis a dramatist and not an essayist. You want your readers to *see* and *hear* your characters in action. Continue writing until you feel exhausted by the effort, and then stop. You may or may not be at the end of the first chapter. It's too soon to tell. Know that you will go back many times and revise this chapter. It may even occur that you change this chapter hugely or even cut it out altogether. No matter. You have taken the first and hardest step. You have actually written fiction! There is no turning back now.

3. Let me give you some hints which you can incorporate into your opening scene or chapter:

> a) Keep your first scene or chapter short. Make it brief enough to be read in a matter of minutes, maybe at most three or four pages long.

> b) Somewhere in the first few pages, intersperse one or two paragraphs of exposition or background about the character(s) which will deepen your reader's appreciation of them. This background usually refers to your major character's past actions or life accomplishments. Do not attempt to summarize personality traits. Show these in action. An example might be:

> "Jonas had worked with Mary on several assignments over at the Executive Office Building and had grown to respect her ability to sway opinions among the key movers and shakers. Once, he'd seen her come up to a certain Southern Senator totally unknown to her. She had taken him by the arm and led him down the hall while whispering in his ear. His sudden belly laugh had echoed through the hallowed halls, stopping passersby in their tracks."

Look for opportunities to add such small passages of dramatized exposition to slowly fill in the elements which create tension for the protagonist. Avoid presenting anything not pertinent to the central conflict and wait to give any biographical information which does not bear on the present moment.

c) Try to add to the reader's impression of your characters with every single action, line of dialogue or object of the setting. Never give a detail just because it would be a realistic part of the scene. Look for chances to take even usually mundane items and imply something unique about them. An example might be:

"Riley took out the cigarette, tapped it on the table and then shrugged, staring at it intensely before returning it to the golden box."

d) Make sure that your opening scene/chapter presents at least *one* mystery to the reader. This mystery should be the first overt indication to the major character that some kind of major conflict exists. It need not be hugely dramatic, but compelling enough to make your reader wonder about it. An example might be:

"Rachel entered her apartment, and as she always did, went routinely to the blinking red light of her answering machine and pushed the play button. She wasn't really listening until she realized whose voice was coming loud and clear into the room. The voice of her dead father!"

e) Try to end your first chapter with something that will make your reader want to read on. This is called a *narrative hook*. If you have presented the first indications of a mystery and created tension as I indicated above, you should end the chapter when the major character faces the necessity of taking action to seek something further to resolve the tensions created.

f) One final hint: do not necessarily go to the next logical scene which is suggested by your opening. It is usually a good idea to hold the tension momentarily and use the chance to offer another, perhaps collateral scene which will apply to the central conflict. Even with first-person or third-person single character points of view, you can delay the expected scene by giving a scene which reveals a new and exciting aspect of the character's life.

STEP NINE

You will revise your novel many times, each time taking advantage of the growing insights you have earned and adding and subtracting things to make your story better. As I said before, it's very possible that your opening scene/chapter will be rewritten or completely changed. This revision will be a necessary and natural part of the creative process. Until you have taken the first step, you cannot take all the others which will eventually bring you to the end of the work. In fact, because you have made these early decisions, your later decisions will be better ones. It's the way human beings have to work. Do not fight against this natural process by stubbornly insisting that your first choices are the best ones. They may be; but they also may not be. Do the best you can in making your first chapter the kind of writing you yourself would want to read. Shape it until you are entirely satisfied with the results. With this highly polished first chapter behind you, you will now have the confidence to go on to subsequent chapters, and each chapter that you finish will give you more and more confidence. You will see the pages piling up and realize that you are working on a project that is possible to complete. Do not worry about the overall quality or publication possibilities. Keep your "eye on the ball." Play the game as intensely as you can; the final score will take care of itself.

Task Summary:

Complete your opening chapter, remembering to incorporate Mystery in the opening paragraphs.

F. Scott Fitzgerald was in debt for most of his life
and died at the age of 44,
thinking himself a failure.

STEP TEN

[The Rest of the Novel]

Task Procedure:

Revise your novel as you write it.

As the pages pile up and chapter after chapter is completed, you might feel many different kinds of emotions. You could feel elated, highly discouraged, cautiously confident, somewhat skeptical, and many other things while the long process of writing a novel unfolds. Know that it is entirely normal to experience a whole gamut of emotions while involved in something as mentally complex and emotionally draining as creating a fictional work. And the problem is compounded by a lack of knowing if what you have created has any merit at all. Usually the last person to be able to judge a piece of writing is the writer him/herself. Writing a novel is analogous in part to the raising of a child. You do the best job you can, and then you have to let it (her/him) go. When you reread your work and attempt to judge its qualities, you will occupy a series of frustrating and contradictory emotional stances. There are some days when every word you've written will sound golden, as if God has given you the gift of the ages. The very next day, these very same words will seem like absolute dross, the most clumsily pathetic and clichéd prose ever produced by humankind. Rest assured that neither reaction is valid. Your writing will be as good as you are capable of producing at this point in your career. You will have written skillfully and clumsily and in every other fashion appropriate to your experience. What you should be concerned with is improvement, not achievement.

Still, there are some things you can do to try to make your novel better *while* you are writing it. Let's go through the major ingredients of the fictional process and discuss these elements.

Character

1. Make sure that your characters (especially the major character) continue to grow as your story progresses. One of the most common flaws in an inferior manuscript is static characterization, people who are the same on page 200 as they were on page 30. Character growth stems from plot complexity, so you will want to make sure that your blocking out produces enough dramatic opportunities for your characters to reveal themselves. As you reread what you have written, continue checking on your characters to see if they are not avoiding possible dramatic confrontations and falling into stereotypical portraits. You should keep an ongoing list of character traits, adding to it as you read each chapter. If you find yourself not adding anything to your lists, go back and reconsider the scenes. Maybe you can add more drama by forcing the action to a greater pitch of tension. I have seen writers avoid the very scenes which were most dramatic because they didn't push the action far enough.

2. Make sure that your major character or protagonist has a recognizable agenda which creates an interesting complexity for the reader to identify with. I've read many scripts which turn the major character into a kind of witness who never makes any choices on his/her own, but who merely reacts to the demands of others. These kind of predictable characters are usually the product of oversimplified plotting and a writer who is only concerned with reporting a series of actions for their own sake. All of your characters require emotional goals of their own which will add conflict to your scenes.

3. Make sure that your cast of characters is as small as possible by continuing to appraise the necessity for their presence in the story. I call this the "paper towel approach." By that I mean, you should use characters over and over again, so that hypothetically, one character might provide three functions in the plot, rather than having three separate characters provide one each. This kind of economy is just another example of fictional compression which is the goal of

the modern novel. Each time a minor character appears in the story, he/she gains in texture and incumbent interest in the reader. A small cast of interesting and intensely drawn characters can greatly enhance your plot. Be careful, however, not to make your minor characters too internally complex because then they will distract from the focus on your major character and confuse your readers' reactions.

Plot

1. Even though you have worked long and hard on your various plot constructions, there are likely to be flaws in your intentions that do not show up until the actual writing begins. Make sure that your plot is constructed of an unbreakable chain of cause-and-effect actions. The issue here is plausibility in two ways. The first is called *realism of action*. Ask yourself—given the criteria of setting which you have created—can your characters plausibly perform all the actions you are asking of them? If you need a six-year-old child to swim a raging river, you are probably stretching plausibility to the breaking point. If your readers question *any* of your characters' actions on this basis, the story will seemed contrived. This sense of contrivance is the reader reaction writers fear the most.

The second kind of plausibility is called *realism of motive*. The question you have to keep asking yourself is *would* your characters perform the actions you are describing, even though they have the physical capacity to do so? Character motivation is an important ingredient of your story and potentially your story's most vulnerable spot. When you portray characters, you are revealing your psychological and emotional knowledge of human beings, and if you reveal yourself as shallow or unintelligent, your novel will cease to interest readers. Obviously, formula novels have less need to reveal this kind of human understanding, but even so, the motives of your characters will inevitably imply the quality of your life experience.

You can help make your novel plausible in both ways by not settling for the first suggestion that comes to mind. The longer you ponder the intangible elements of your characters' personalities and resultant actions, the more subtle will be your conception of them as people. The biographies you did earlier will help a great deal in this regard. You may also have to do considerable research to make sure that all of your facts are accurate and up-to-date. I knew a writer who read ten books on armored warfare, and ended up using only *one* detail about tanks in his novel! Obviously, the longer and deeper you have lived, the more this issue will work to your advantage. Remember that nothing is ever lost on you. Even the most trivial bit of life experience might someday be of use to you in presenting one of your characters.

2. Make sure that there are never any long lapses in tension in your story. Such lapses come when a story is biding its time, setting up future conflicts. Two ways to avoid these gaps are by creating *different level priorities* and by using subplots.

A writer prioritizes by relating only those things which create drama in the scene or summary. Mainly, the writer has no trouble rendering those aspects of character, plot and setting which dominate at any given time. These key actions are first-level priorities. If these first-level elements are not immediately tension-building, invent a temporary issue for the length of that scene only. This issue could be some aspect of character, plot, or setting which can "entertain" the reader while the first level material is being read. One of my students wrote a scene which necessitated the major character's being visited in jail by another witness character who filled him in on what was happening in the outside world. The first level purpose of this scene was primarily informational. I suggested that the writer create a second level priority, a momentary point of interest to keep the reader involved while the information was being presented. The writer placed a sleeping cell mate in the scene and a cockroach slowly crawling toward the open mouth of this snoring cell mate! The outcome of this event was enough to keep the reader entertained and not aware of the writer's primary purpose with the scene. Of course, the incident was not just there to entertain. It also offered a symbolic comment on the essential plot situation in which the major character was involved.

Subplots have been mentioned before. They can achieve many things in deepening the readers' appreciation of your story. If you use the omniscient third-person point of view, you can achieve a kind of "bonus" tension by creating dramatic scenes in which the major character is not present. Don't forget that there are two overall ways to have tension attach itself to a protagonist. One comes from the major character's own awareness of what is wrong or problematical. A second method creates additional story lines which show a pending problem to the reader but not to the major character. A person may be trying to negotiate the boiling rapids of a river in a kayak and have his/her hands filled with the tensions of the moment. You, the viewer of this drama, would have your enjoyment of this scene increased even more if you were told that a half mile down stream and out of sight from the character was a gigantic waterfall that would soon threaten the character's life. No matter how many subplots you invent, remember to make sure that they are a natural part of the overall central conflict and eventually merge with the main plot line while creating a series of mini climaxes of their own.

3. Make sure that there are no redundancies of scene or summary in your overall plot. My first novel involved a character in three long episodes. They all might have been interesting on their own, but the latter two did not add anything new to the readers' knowledge of my major character. My novel was much like a television series which, of course, is not trying to end! Make sure that each and every scene or chapter *advances* the story in some kind of new way toward the climax. Never relate the same kind of scene with the same kind of characters more than once. This principle relates to even very minor actions unless the repetition is being used to make a special point about the characters involved. I recently read a novel in which the protagonist, an amateur detective, kept going back to the same place to interview the same person several times. Each time, the character being questioned added something new to the overall inquiry. I pointed out to the writer that all three of these scenes could be compressed into one, and that time could be passed in more efficient ways than rendering the same scene over and over.

4. Potentially, there are as many kinds of writing styles as there are writers, so I certainly cannot in any way attempt to discuss or even mention all of them here. Likewise, many apparent deviations from traditional style usages are performed by writers who know what they're doing. The only real issue in the application of any fiction writing technique is whether it works to better dramatize the story along the lines that the writer desires. However, given the difficult publication world today, and the normal demands of story, I think that your readers *deserve to know what's happening in your story.* Make sure that there is enough exposition of background information and other important factual material, so that your readers can appreciate what's at stake in the major character's life. Many times, inexperienced writers try to be so subtle that they keep from

the reader the necessary ingredients of the characters' lives. The result is confusion or boredom, and neither reaction invites the reader to become involved in your novel. There's an old saying in writing circles: don't be cute with the facts. There are times when purposeful ambiguity will serve a dramatic purpose. But make sure that your readers understand the basic situation which will dramatize the mystery, suspense and surprise necessary for overall reader participation. Once you have hooked the reader, you can remember to keep a balance of explicitness and implicitness which is appropriate to your type of novel.

5. While you are writing your novel, check for varieties of pace and tone. Some of the best novels can be ruined by too much of a good thing. Novels dealing with adventure and suspense are especially prone to this problem. Writers who have been trained to work from an intricate blocking out sometimes forget that their readers like and need an occasional rest from the constant tensions presented by the story. Pace should generally start out fast in the beginning, slow down and go through various speedups during the length of the story, and then end with a rush. There are naturally many variations from this standard procedure, so that you need to understand your particular manuscript and respond to pace accordingly.

Tone is somewhat more subtle because it deals with the emotional intangibilities of subject matter, so that any "rules" for its handling are not easily cited. Even the most serious or tragic work can hopefully illustrate moments of humor, as similarly, the most ribald farce is inevitably reflective of much more serious matters. You need to feel deeply enough about your characters' motives to see the contrasting emotions present in their actions. Again, subplots can offer a welcome tonal respite from any kind of relentless pursuit of only one side of the emotional coin. For example, Fitzgerald uses Gatsby's big party scene and Nick Carraway's gentle narrative voice to soften what would otherwise be an overwhelming view of the inherent tragedy he's presenting.

6. The climax of your story is extremely important and should be derived more-or-less naturally from the events that lead up to it. This inevitability may have surprise twists, but should still seem appropriate to the plot structure, a final piece in the

puzzle as it were. It will sometimes be the case that you don't know how your book will end until you get there. But know that you are open to those discoveries which will take into account all that you have done up to that point. Try not to conceive of arbitrary or oversimplified endings which make your story trite or superficial. Let the ending evolve, as you have all the parts of your story. Writers often make the crucial mistake of being impatient to finish their work. Here most of all is where you need to take your time and think/feel out the events of your novel. It's probably true that most publishers want so-called happy endings, but you must make sure that your ending is true to your characters and your vision of them. Otherwise, the supposed "happy" ending won't be happy because it will seem contrived and false. D. H. Lawrence used a phrase in much of his work which is appropriate to this issue. He called it "a character turn." This phrase is primarily stated metaphorically and implies that there will come a certain moment in your major character's life when he/she will "turn" and realize the fatality of his/her actions. In other words, the ending has been reached. This concept recognizes what is most important about a novel's climax—that it should be dramatic to the very last word. There are epilogues and other kind of anticlimaxes in even modern stories, but I think you will be best served if you recognize the need for a taut ending and not let your story escape into a generalized commentary.

Setting

1. Although most publishers will tell you that they don't like scripts with too much setting, I think what they're saying is that they don't like stories with setting poorly written. Sense of place can give your novel that special, piquant flavor to lift it above the mundane and the clichéd. Certainly, Fitzgerald's special talent with description, to a large extent, makes *The Great Gatsby* a compelling work. Writers sometimes are in a hurry to relate their plot actions and bypass moments in their stories in which setting could be better exploited. Be alert to those places where a few details of place can pull in the reader and make your characters' actions all the more meaningful.

2. Make sure that you have not related setting details for the mere sake of doing so. This kind of "showing off" (sometimes called

local color) generally detracts from a novel because it makes the reader too much aware of you the author. Especially when using exotic or unusual settings, will you be "invited" to overwrite setting details and try to "prove" your knowledge of the locale. Remember that like all fictional techniques, setting should serve the plot and the major character's central conflict, not your own ego.

3. Remember to found all scenes in time and place. Many writers fall into the expository habit of relating their characters' actions in a kind of setting void, not placing them in detailed locations. This lack of setting materialization makes the actions seem to "float free" in a sea of words. Summary passages are the most common culprits. They allow a writer to lapse into an overly general rendition of his/her characters' actions without telling the reader when and where these actions are happening. It takes very few words to accomplish this important task: "It was the next morning at the stable that Mary confronted John." This single sentence can make all the difference in making your reader feel a part of the events you are relating.

4. Like your characters, your setting also needs to grow in your readers' minds. Don't go back to the same place without a good plot reason, but if you have to, remember to add details not given before. Use these details to create the new tensions you are dramatizing between your characters. As you know, setting itself can be used as one of the primary antagonists in your story. In such cases, you will need to make sure that you are conceiving of your settings in the most intimate way possible. Although these settings will ultimately remain secondary in importance, they can be wonderful catalysts in the formation of tension elements and even the central conflict itself. A great part of *The Great Gatsby*'s success is achieved by Fitzgerald's use of setting. A helpful exercise would be for you to list all the elements in this novel which could not be removed without considerably hurting the story. Such concentrations on any one element are not accidental. They are present in a work because they were needed. Analyzing their usage can teach you how to apply the device to your work.

Point of View

1. The major question is whether your original choice of point

of view was the right one. Once you get into the actual writing, be alert to any signals your characters start giving you. To some extent, having the right point of view is a matter of feel. Does the narrative sound right? Are you unduly restricted in being able to relate what you have to, in the way you want to? Perhaps first-person point of view is restricting your manipulation of the plot. Maybe the third-person omniscient is creating too much distance in what is essentially an intimate, one-person story. You will want to be consistent to whatever choice you made, but not arbitrarily. Once you have written a few chapters, go back over them and see if the point of view was somehow harming your ability to render the events. If so, then change the point of view to that which gives you the most advantages and least disadvantages and rewrite that portion accordingly.

2. Another important issue of point of view is aesthetic distance. Even within the point of view choice, you may still be keeping the reader too close or too far away from the characters' actions. This factor is difficult to judge without considerable writing experience, but you can develop a sense for the key moments in your story and where you want the reader to be. Remember that you can also vary the distance by the type and amount of details you use, and when and how long you involve your characters in close-up scenes. You will want to vary the distance in response to what is going on in your story. A cross-country plane trip might take you two or three paragraphs of skillfully detailed summary, whereas a key love scene might take several pages. Mostly, it's a matter of logic, but become aware of what's happening to your characters' emotions, so that you can find the best place to be at any given time.

3. Although internal revelation of a character's thoughts and feelings tends to make your readers feel closer to those characters (and thus shrink the aesthetic distance), the balance between external and internal revelation must always be kept in mind. This usage will, of course, reflect your overall style and voice, but it also needs to be given some thought. A scene may call for a heavy percentage of external details: a character is fleeing through a city street. Or it may call for a high percentage of internal details: a character is contemplating a beautiful sight. Whatever degree of external or internal details you pick, remember that your story will thrive best when it is shown and not told. Try to have faith in your reader and

allow your characters' outward lives to imply the internal factors you want them to. Newer writers tend to talk about their characters more than show them in action, thinking that this straight forward presentation will make them more interesting to readers. Ironically, most of the time, the reverse is true. The issue goes back to what a story is—a series of experiences which are lived via the five senses. Meaning or feeling will only come across if these experiences are *first* lived, and *then* understood. Think about this: when you were born, would you have liked someone to come in and tell you what your life was going to be about, instead of allowing you live it on your own? Well, your readers want to make the same choice. Give them a cogent story with an abundance of external details, and they will contribute the desired meaning you're so concerned about "getting across." Perhaps Henry James, the great British writer, said it best. "I will sometimes tell you what my characters are thinking, but I will never tell you why."

Revision

Of course, as I indicated above, you will be revising your novel as you write it, and there are several general ways to accomplish this important task. You can revise what you wrote the day before. You can wait to revise various parts, perhaps individual episodes or chapters. Or you can wait to revise the whole novel after completing a first draft. Hopefully, you have been modifying your initial concepts all along, as your awareness of what you were doing matured, and you learned more about the process. As I have already indicated several times, the writing process works best in a constant state of calm and patient reexamination. Most successful writers would probably agree that they never felt that their novels were finished to an absolute perfection. Perhaps there is no such thing in any human endeavor. But you need to persevere your efforts to a point where you feel you are no longer capable of improving what you have done. You will know when that point is reached. The same Muse that has been helping you through the whole procedure will whisper those magic words, "it's done," and you will begin to transfer your attention to that next project which has probably already started to take seed in your mind and heart. So you have now reached that point when the book is essentially done, and it's time to do a final in-depth revision before submitting your work to anyone's review—either to an interested reader or a professional agent or publisher. The following are aspects of this final revision:

The Overall Plot Structure

Page through the novel and make sure that each and every action proceeds naturally and interestingly from the preceding one. Try to get that feel that you want the reader to have, that of a gradually growing tension and inevitability. Make sure that there are no lapses, no loopholes where the reader can escape into skepticism or boredom. Check to see that every plot action is absolutely necessary, is not redundant to any other, and is inevitably leading to the next. Finally, make sure that the story ends with a bang, leaving the reader hungry for more.

The Characters' Motivations

Again go through your book, examining the motives of the characters (especially the protagonist and key antagonists), testing them against what is both plausible and true to human psychology as you know it. Ferret out any character actions which are arbitrary or forced. See if the major character's motives grow as the novel does, always deepening the reader's appreciation and involvement. Check to see if you have derived every possible moment of tension from your characters' interactions. For example, perhaps you have avoided a promising scene between character A and character B or not made them push hard enough for what they themselves want to obtain. Especially notice their dialogues and cut out all over-explicitness which gives away the latent tensions driving them. Imply their motivations through their speeches and actions, making the reader wonder why they are performing as they are, and then provide the answers by further external presentations. Finally, check for any inconsistencies of motive when a character might act inexplicably or arbitrarily to serve some temporary or expedient plot purpose.

The Researchable Facts

Check out every citation of time and place and make sure that it is factually accurate. You may be using an overall fictional context which allows you great latitude in the naming of things, but wherever you are relying on actuality, you need to be absolutely true to what is real and factual, especially historically. Also check your background research to insure enough specificity of description to serve the needs of the characters involved. A deliberately vague or ambiguous reference can take away from the overall authenticity of your work and weaken the plot. Always base your naming process on what is most factually useful to your dramatic purpose and do not invent names just for the sake of doing so.

So now you're ready to submit your work for publication, get published, become famous and make lots of money! Well, not quite!

It is a good idea to first search out readers as preliminary judges or critics of your novel before submitting it to professional agents or publishers. These readers could be friends who have an interest in your subject matter or in reading in general. They might be writing instructors from classes you have taken or professional writing consultants or "book doctors" who are themselves professional teachers and writers. If you can, try to get a variety of readers who will represent different perspectives on both the content and style of your work. Regardless if they are professional readers or not, offer to pay them with money or services you can offer them. Some expense at this point will be well worth it. Once you have received these responses, consider them carefully and weigh each of the reactions against the others. Do not automatically make any changes based only on these readings, but at the same time, realize that they may be offering you some excellent ideas that you can use to make your novel better. Adopt an attitude of open consideration, and remember that there are many avenues of insight which may come your way, not all wonderful, not all useful, some perhaps even harmful, but still perhaps some, maybe only one, that might make all the difference. If you do adopt any of the changes suggested by these readers, remember that any change you make will affect everything else in the story, so that one change might create the need for several others. Constantly review the whole novel with every individual adaptation and run through the revisionary items mentioned above to make sure that they are working as they were before.

A hard truth to realize (especially when you're somewhat inexperienced) is that sometimes you will be called upon to make major revisions of your story. I know a writer who took another year and a half with what she thought was a finished work because one professional reviewer saw major flaws in the major character concept, and the writer realized that the criticism was valid. Any time you take in the revising of your novel—when you realize that it is necessary—will be time well spent. Remember, your novel, when finally completed, will be in that form forever. It is doubtful that you will ever go back to it again once time has elapsed. Make it as good as you can now, and it will make you happy for the rest of your life.

Task Summary:

> **Complete your novel, keeping in mind the following things:**
>
> **That your Characters grow from complexity and are few in number.**
>
> **That your Plot structure has plausibility, varieties of tone and pace, second-level prioritizing, and a suitable climax; and that it does not repeat itself.**
>
> **That your Setting's sense of place grows in the reader's mind, is founded in time and place and does not suffer from an effect of local color.**
>
> **That your Point of View allows for effective dramatization, varieties of aesthetic distance and a balance between internal and external rendering of details.**
>
> *And finally that* **your last revision checks your Plot structure, your Characters' motivations and all of the researchable facts.**

Good luck!

Appendix A

Marketing Your Novel

Publication of a novel today is an extremely hard task to accomplish, no matter who you are. But if you are a first time novelist and unpublished, the task is nearly impossible. Having said that, let's try to achieve the impossible!

First, remember that you are writing a novel because you want to reach an audience. You have planned your entire writing process to suit that audience. How do you reach them? There are several ways, and you need to practice them all simultaneously and continuously. If you are trying to market your novel and relying upon its publication for monetary or emotional support, you are probably destined to be disappointed. You have to go about the procedure with a professional, workman like attitude, and you must never give up. You need to do the following things:

1. Obtain a good, professional agent. There are hundreds of good agents in New York City and elsewhere. There may even be some in your hometown. You can obtain their names from the telephone directory, from writing organizations, from writing instructors, from advertisements in newspapers and magazines, from friends who are writers, and from books. Perhaps the most popular books are *Writer's Market*, *The Literary Market Place*, and *Literary Agents of North America*. To be most effective, network all personal contacts which can connect you with agents. Agents are just like we are. They are more likely to pay attention to someone who has come recommended than to someone they do not know.

One word of warning! Do not deal with "agents" who offer to read your manuscript for a large fee. Most literary agents do not charge for their initial reading of your materials (see below for the procedure of submission). Those who ask for flat fees in the hundred of dollars, or worse, prorated fees for numbers of words or pages, are probably not true literary agents. They are reading services which may or may not help you. Their main way of making money is by charging you for reading your novel, not by selling it to a publisher. You have to be very careful and first investigate the credentials of any agent who wants to charge you a fee. You have every right to ask for a list of recent successes or the names of writers who have been represented. At the very least, send out only a few pages and see what is provided you in the way of response.

Once you have determined that there are several agents who have an interest and expertise in your type of novel, send them all the following: a) a *very brief* cover letter naming your novel and its genre and asking the agent to consider representing you; b) an author's sheet which is a brief summary of your novel's greatest selling points and a short biography of yourself (sample below); c) a self-addressed, stamped envelope (SASE) for their response. If you have gained the agent's name through some personal contact, then, of course, mention that fact in the cover letter. If that person recommends your novel in some way, also mention that. Also, at the end of your cover letter, you might ask for any names of agents that this particular agent might recommend, if he/she is not interested in seeing your work.

If one or more of these solicited agents asks to see parts or all of your novel, follow their instructions to the letter, again remembering to include suitable return postage and/or a stamped envelop large enough to accommodate your manuscript. If an agent rejects your novel but makes suggestions about it, consider them carefully, and perhaps incorporate them into another revision before submitting your novel again. If you are lucky enough to be approved for representation, read your contract carefully or take it to a lawyer who is familiar with literary contracts.

2. Network every possible lead in obtaining a publisher for your novel. Most publishers today will not read unrepresented manuscripts. They do not have the staff necessary to screen the high number of novels that are sent them. However, a few companies are still somewhat open to "over the transom" manuscripts. To find out their names, consult one of several books which list publishers and their policies regarding submissions. Networking means being aggressive in contacting teachers, writing consultants, friends, business associates, relatives, anyone with even a peripheral association with a publishing company. You might be able to contact the friend of a friend of a friend. Some people even attempt to contact other, well known writers, but this procedure usually does not work and might even alienate part of the publication world against you. Ken Kesey, the writer of *One Flew Over the Cuckoo's Nest*, marketed his book in New York, by going from door to door requesting a

personal interview. Not all of you have the means or the capacity to do this, but it does imply to what lengths writers have gone to get noticed. Again, you have to be perseverant and not take no for an answer, but simultaneously be open to the incorporation of useful criticism into a revision of your present work and the writing of future books. I have noticed that most successful writers are very open people. They will generally welcome the advice of others in the continuation of their growth process as artists.

3. *If you have large financial resources*, you might want to take advantage of a new publishing alternative, called "Co-Publishing." This method differs in several ways from what has been called the "Vanity Press" method. First, you pay fifty per cent (not a hundred) of the publication costs, and the publisher pays the other fifty per cent. You also share in any royalties on the same fifty-fifty basis. In contrast to the typical vanity publisher, this arrangement gives the co-publisher an incentive to publicize your work, and also the means to do so. Most co-publishers also have conventional publication facilities, and as a result, have the necessary means to sell your novel to all the major markets. You can obtain a list of such co-publishers from *Publisher's Weekly* in New York City.

Remember that publication of your novel, as wonderful and necessary as it is, is not the final warranting of your efforts and expertise. I could cite countless examples of very fine novels and novelists who were not published in their initial attempts. Some world class writers, alas, have even gone unrecognized during their lifetimes, only to be discovered years or decades later. Ultimately, you cannot control the opinions and actions of those in charge of the publication system. "All" you can do is write the best book you can and never give up trying to write a better one. If you do this and never publish a book, you will at least know that the process itself has been worthy of your efforts, and you worthy of it.

Sample Author's Sheet

The Great Gatsby is a novel about a country and its times and what both did to the hopes and dreams of those idealists who still dared to strive within its borders. The major character, Jay Gatsby, has become rich through illicit means, but still seeks the one thing that has eluded him, the love of his life, a young woman who wouldn't marry him when he was a penniless nobody. Still his obsession seems near to being fulfilled when the young woman is presented to him via a series of surprising, yet menacing circumstances. Neither the woman herself nor those who surround him are capable of matching the major character's capacity for romantic illusion, so within the seed of his hope lies the flower of his destruction. But Gatsby is more than a story of one man's powerful dream. It is a story of a generation whose mountainous indulgence in pleasure made it insensitive to even its own best members. This novel strikes to the sentimental core in all of us while simultaneously portraying our own potential for cruel disregard. Only the narrator Nick Carraway survives intact to fight another day, somewhat sadder, somewhat wiser, wounded but not bowed, like its author perhaps.

F. SCOTT FITZGERALD is one of America's greatest young writers. His work has set a high standard for American letters. Among his publications are, *This Side of Paradise* and *Tender Is the Night*, plus many short stories which deal with the American Jazz Age. They are written with lyrical beauty and a haunting sense of what-might-have-been. His work deals with characters who are seeking the impossible, but who refuse to recognize their inability to achieve it.

Appendix B
Bibliography

Aristotle, *The Rhetoric and the Poetics*, Modern Library, Random House, New York, 1954.

Beach, Joseph Warren, *Twentieth Century Novel*: Studies in Technique, Appleton-Century, 1932.

Bellamy, Joe David, *The New Fiction: Interviews with Innovative American Writers*, University of Illinois Press, Urbana, Chicago and London, 1974.

Block, Lawrence, *Writing the Novel: from Plot to Print*, Writer's Digest Books, Cincinnati, Ohio, 1979.

Booth, Wayne C., *The Rhetoric of Fiction*, University of Chicago Press, 1961.

Bowen, Elizabeth, *Collected Impressions*, Knopf, 1950.

Brande, Dorothea, *Becoming a Writer*, J. P. Tarcher, Inc. distributed by Houghton Mifflin Company, Boston, 1981.

Brohaugh, William, *The Writer's Resource Guide*, Writer's Digest Books, Cincinnati, Ohio, 1979.

Brooks, Cleanth, Jr. and Warren, Robert Penn, *Understanding Fiction*, second edition, Appleton-Century-Croft, 1959.

Burroway, Janet, *Writing Fiction: a Guide to Narrative Craft*, Little, Brown, Boston, 1982.

Cary, Joyce, *Art and Reality*, Cambridge University Press, Doubleday Anchor, 1958.

Cassill, R. V., *Writing Fiction*, Prentice-Hall, Inc., Englewood Cliffs, New Jersey, 1975.

Cather, Willa, *On Writing: Critical Studies on Writing as an Art*, Knopf, 1949.

Cox, Sidney, *Indirections - for those who want to write*, Nonpareil Books, David R. Godine, Boston, 1981.

Daiches, David, *The Novel and the Modern World*, University of Chicago Press, 1960.

Dickson, Frank A. and Smythe, Sandra, *Handbook of Short Story Writing*, Writer's Digest Books, Cincinnati, Ohio, 1971.

Forster, E. M., *Aspects of the Novel*, Harvest, Harcourt, Brace & Jovanovich, Inc., New York, 1927.

Gardner, John, *On Becoming a Novelist*, Harper & Row, New York, 1983.
Goodman, Paul, *The Structure of Literature*, University of Chicago Press, 1954.
Gordon, Caroline, *How to Read a Novel*, Viking, 1957.
Hayakawa, S. I., *Language in Thought and Action*, fourth edition, Harcourt Brace & Jovanovich, Inc., New York, 1941.
Hoover, Carol, *How To Write An Uncommonly Good Novel*, Ariadne, Rockville, Maryland, 1990.
Humphrey, Robert, *Stream of Consciousness in the Modern Novel*, University of California Press, Berkeley and Los Angeles, 1962.
Hutchinson, Peter, *Games Authors Play*, Methuen, New York and London, 1983.
James, Henry, *The Art of Fiction, and Other Essays*, ed. Morris Roberts, Oxford University Press, 1948.
James, Henry, *The Art of the Novel*: Critical Prefaces, Scribner's, 1934.
Levin, Harry, *Symbolism and Fiction*, University of Virginia Press, Charlottesville, 1956.
Lubbock, Percy, *The Craft of Fiction*, Scribner's, 1921.
Lucas, F. L., *Style*, Macmillan: Collier Books, New York, 1962.
Lukacs, Georg, *The Theory of the Novel*, The MIT Press, Cambridge, Massachusetts, 1971.
Macaulay, Robie and Lanning, George, *Technique in Fiction*, Harper and Row, 1964.
Martin, Harold Clark, *Styles in Prose Fiction*, Columbia University Press, 1959.
Meredith, Robert C., and Fitzgerald, John D., *Structuring Your Novel: From Basic Idea to Finished Manuscript*, Barnes & Noble Books, a Division of Harper & Row, New York, 1972.
Miles, Josephine, *Style and Proportion: the Language of Prose and Poetry*, Little Brown, Boston, 1967.
Munson, Gorham Bert, *Style and Form in American Prose*, Kennikat Press, Port Washington, New York, 1969.
Percy, Walker, *The Message in the Bottle*, Farrar, Straus and Giroux, New York, 1954.
Plimpton, George, and Cowley, Malcolm (First Series), *The Paris Review Interviews: Writers at Work, Series One-Five*, Penguin Books, various dates.

Plimpton, George, *The Writer's Chapbook: a Compendium of Fact, Opinion, Wit, and Advice from the 20th Century's Preeminent Writers*, Viking, 1989.

Queneau, Raymond, *Exercises in Style*, New Directions, New York, 1981.

Robbe-Grillet, Alain, *For a New Novel: Essays on Fiction*, trans. by Richard Howard, Grove Press, 1965.

Schorer, Mark, "Technique as Discovery," Hudson Review, Spring, 1948.

Sloane, William, *The Craft of Writing*, Norton, New York, 1983.

Spiegel, Alan, *Fiction and the Camera Eye: visual consciousness in film and the modern novel*, University Press of Virginia, Charlottesville, 1976.

Surmelian, Leon, *Techniques of Fiction Writing*, Doubleday Anchor, New York, 1969.

Wellek, Rene and Warren, Austin, *Theory of Literature*, Harcourt, Brace, 1956.

Welty, Eudora, *One Writer's Beginnings*, Warner Books, New York, 1983.

Wharton, Edith, *The Writing of Fiction*, Scribner's, New York, 1925.

Appendix C

Glossary

Abstract Words:	Words which represent concepts or feelings
Action:	An act performed by a fictional character
Advance	Release of new information about the characters
Aesthetic Distance	Human recognition of the artistic aspects of something
Antagonist	A minor character who provokes or incites conflict for the major character
Atmosphere	The emotional quality of a setting (also called mood)
Blocking Out	The systematic planning of a fictional work, especially its plot
Camera Eye	A point of view which renders events only through the presentation of external details (also called effaced narrator)
Characterization	The process of portraying characters via their physical appearance, actions, dialogues, settings, and thoughts and feelings
Chronological Time	Events follow one after another in a logical sequence, as in Monday, Tuesday, Wednesday
Climax	That point in a plot where the main or central conflict is resolved or ended
Compression	Methods used to dramatize elements of character, plot and setting which use the fewest amount of words and space
Concrete Words	Words which represent things that have physical mass or which appeal to one of the five senses

Conflict	Elements in a fictional piece which create stress or frustration in the characters' lives
Central	The main problem of the major character in a work of fiction
External	Physical causes of stress like people, places and things
Internal	Subjective causes of stress like thoughts and feelings
Cumulative Structure	An arrangement of plot actions, none of which is enough meaningful on its own to create a complete story
Denouement	The part of the plot that follows the climax (also called falling action or anticlimactic)
Dialogue	The fictional representation of human speech
Effaced Narrator	A point of view which renders events via the presentation of only external details (also called camera eye)
Epilogue	That portion of a novel which follows the climax in the plot, usually briefly
Episodic Structure	An arrangement of plot actions which are generally capable of standing on their own in forming a meaningful story
Exposition	Those passages in a fictional work which serve to present information about the characters more or less directly to the reader
Falling Action	The part of the plot that follows the climax (also called anticlimactic)
Flashback	Rendering that portion of a character's life which precedes the start of the novel in terms of time
Flash Forward	That portion of the plot that moves ahead of the time period being rendered at any given moment
Flat Character	A character (usually easily recognizable) whose function in a

	fictional work is to create tension/conflict for the major character (also called a minor character)
Half Scene	A temporary interruption of a summary passage via the use of a few details of presentation
Local Color	The presentation of an excessive amount of setting details for a purpose not connected with the central conflict
Major Character	The person in a fictional work whose function it is to demonstrate the central conflict - the person through whom the reader experiences the most intimate parts of the story (also called protagonist)
Materialization	That construction in a reader's mind that approximates the presentation of physical or external details dedicated to create an image of actual experience
Minor Character	A character (usually easily recognizable) whose function in a fictional work is to create tension/conflict for the major character (also called flat character)
Mood	The emotional quality of a setting (also called atmosphere)
Motif	That general human motive which appears over and over to motivate a fictional character - an example would be revenge
Motive	That specific human reason which makes a character do or not do something - an example would be a character's wanting to revenge the killing of a loved one
Muse	That inner voice who provides a variety of creative projects
Mystery	A universal life element which bases its effect on our not knowing something we want to know

Objective Time	A naturalistic rendering of time which is measured by mechanical objects like a clock - it is always of the same duration no matter how it is measured or what it is named
Pace	The amount of words or space on the page used in proportion to the amount of information presented to a reader - scene creates a slow pace and summary creates a fast pace
Physical Appearance	Those aspects of a character's body which contribute to a story's effectiveness
Physical Backdrops	Aspects of a setting which create the illusion of a specific place
Plot (Structure)	The presentation and sequencing of cause and effect based actions which dramatize the major character's central conflict, mainly through external means
Main Plot	The dominant series of actions
Subplot	The secondary series of actions
Plot Shape	Those basic, primitive life situations which appear again and again in human affairs - an example would be search
Point of View	Use of character's subjective impressions in rendering a story
First Person	Use of the "I" voice when referencing the point of view character(s)
Third Person	Use of "he" or "she" voice when referencing the point of view of character(s) - examples include single character or limited
Omniscient	Use of two or more characters' impressions in rendering a story (via "he" or "she referencing)
Premise	A brief presentation of the basic situation via which the mystery, suspense and surprise will be dramatized

Protagonist	The person in a fictional work whose function it is to demonstrate the central conflict - the person through whom the reader experiences the most intimate parts of the story (also called major character)
Realism	A literary movement which emphasizes the writer's use of actual, everyday elements in a story
Referencing	Use of a particular pronoun to refer to a character in a story
Rising Action	Those actions in a plot which precede the climax (also called period of complication)
Scene	A detailed presentation of character actions via the use of details of dialogue, action, setting, physical appearance and thoughts and feelings
Sense of Place	The emotions connected with a particular place which are represented via the details of choice
Setting	The elements of time and place which function to provide the stage on which the characters' actions occur
Stream of Consciousness	The presentation of a character's thoughts and feelings more or less directly from the character's mind
Style	The choices a writer makes when applying fiction writing techniques
Subjective Time	An internal rendering of time as it is affected by a character's awareness of what is happening around him/her (also called experiential time)
Subsequent Action	The choosing of an action far down the line in a series of action which implies the occurrence of those preceding it
Summary	The rendering of fictional elements to cover distances of time and space via the choice of a few details to imply many

Surprise	The presentation of events in a plot which are not expected
Suspense	The human emotion which is created when a sympathetic character is acting at risk - it is characterized by the reader's wanting to know what is going to happen next in a story
Symbolic Action	The presentation of a character act which implies significant meanings beyond those normally associated with the act
Symbolism	A literary technique which uses life elements to represent meanings not normally associated with the elements in terms of type or degree
Tension Elements	Those specific items in the life of a character which cause conflict
Time Patter	An organization of the sequencing of character actions in a certain recognizable form
Time Zone	The length of time used from the start to the end of the story
Tone	A writer's emotional attitude which is implied through his/her choices of subject matter and the application of the fictional techniques
Typical Action	The rendering of character actions which imply a frequency of repetition over a period of time

Index

Abstract words 9
Aesthetic distance 65
Alice In Wonderland 55
Antagonist 12, 32, 43, 45, 51, 61, 96, 99
Aristotle 16
Baker, Jordan 48, 52, 61, 78
Blocking out 48, 60, 61, 63, 69, 70, 73, 77, 78, 79, 82, 84, 90, 94
Book doctor 78, 100
Buchanan, Daisy 28, 32, 50, 61, 66
Buchanan, Tom 35, 48, 52, 56, 62
Camera Eye 75
Carraway, Nick 32, 33, 48, 50, 75, 76, 94
Catcher In the Rye 28
Central conflict 16, 28, 33, 39, 43, 44, 45, 47, 49, 60, 61, 62, 68, 70, 81, 82, 85, 86, 93, 96, 112, 114
Characterization 19, 90
Charles Dickens 21
Chatterley, Constance 44
Climax 16, 28, 35, 56, 58, 93, 94, 95
Compression 57, 71, 90
Concrete words 9, 10
Conrad, Joseph 13, 16
Cumulative structure 56
de Stendhal 21
Dialogue 19, 59, 77, 84, 86, 99
Dickinson, Emily 25
Effaced Narrator 75
Episodic structure 56
Exposition 20, 85, 93
External conflict 16
Falling action 16, 17
Fielding, Henry 21
First-person 22, 23, 33, 40, 45, 50, 66, 67, 73, 74, 75, 76, 86, 97
Fitzgerald, F. Scott 5, 28, 61, 78, 81, 88
Flashback 68
Flaubert, Gustave 21
Forster, E. M. 14

Gatsby, Jay 28, 31, 76
Great Gatsby, The 5, 28, 29, 30, 33, 50, 52, 53, 55, 56, 61, 66, 70, 75, 76, 81, 95, 96
Half-scene 58
Hardy, Thomas 10
Hawthorne, Nathaniel 21
Huckleberry Finn 21
Iago 45
Internal conflict 16, 76
Kesey, Ken 104
Lady Chatterley's Lover 44
Lawrence, D. H. 13, 80, 95
Local color 96, 101
Lord Jim 16
Madame Bovary 21
Main plot 47, 48, 51, 52, 53, 60, 61, 93
Major character 12, 13, 14, 16, 17, 18, 19, 27, 28, 29, 30, 31, 32, 33, 40, 42, 43, 44, 45, 60, 68, 76, 81, 84, 86, 90, 92, 93, 95, 96, 99, 101
Mark Twain 21
Materialization 11, 74, 96
Mellors 44
Minor character 32, 37, 43, 44, 45, 47, 48, 51, 52, 60 61, 70, 74, 76, 81, 91
Mood 12
Motif 27, 28, 29, 31
Motive 16, 18, 26, 28, 29, 31, 32, 39, 40, 45, 51, 52, 56, 77, 91, 94, 99
Muse 5, 98
Mystery 15, 16, 29, 34, 37, 49, 50, 82, 83, 87, 94
Omniscient 66, 75, 92, 97
One Flew Over the Cuckoo's Nest 104
Othello 44, 45
Pace 59, 65, 71, 81, 94, 101
Passage to India 14
Physical appearance 19, 77
Picasso, Pablo 39
Plot Shape 32
Poetics 16
Premise 28, 29, 33, 35, 39, 47, 51, 60, 62, 70, 81
Princess, The 13
Protagonist 31, 38, 44, 51, 85, 90, 92, 99

Realism 21, 76, 91
Red and the Black, The 21
Referencing 22, 66, 67
Richardson, Samuel 21
Rising action 16
Salinger, J. D. 28
Scarlet Letter, The 21
Scene 12, 13, 49, 51, 56, 58, 59, 61, 62, 63, 65, 67, 68, 69, 71, 75, 77, 82, 84, 85, 86, 87, 92, 93, 94, 97, 99
Sense of place 12, 13, 95, 101
Setting 11, 12, 13, 14, 19, 23, 27, 33, 48, 56, 68, 77, 81, 82, 86, 91, 92, 95, 96
Shakespeare 45, 71, 82
Stream of consciousness 20
Style 8, 10, 81, 97, 100
Subjective time 68
Summary 5, 27, 28, 56, 57, 58, 59, 63, 65, 67, 69, 71, 73, 78, 82, 92, 93, 96, 97, 104
Surprise 15, 16, 29, 34, 35, 37, 49, 82, 83, 94
Suspense 15, 16, 29, 34, 37, 49, 50, 82, 83, 94
Symbolic Action 57
Tension elements 29, 34, 52, 84, 96
Thackeray, William 21
Third-person 22, 23, 66, 73, 74, 75, 86, 92, 97
Time pattern 69
Time zone 68
Tolstoy, Leo 3
Tone 70, 71, 94, 101
Typical Action 57
War and Peace 3
Wilson, George B. 52, 56
Wilson, Myrtle 52, 56

The author, Peter Porosky, is a freelance writer, college teacher and writing consultant. His novel *The Sins of Major Lord* was a best seller in West Germany. He has published two other text/trade books, *How To Find Your Own Voice: a Guide to Literary Style*, and *How to Fix Fiction*. In addition, he has published numerous short stories, poems and articles in various magazines and literary journals. He was also editor of Signet's *The Erotic Anthology*. He lives in Germantown, Maryland, with his wife Linda and teaches at the University of Maryland.